DOING THE WORK OF THE EVANGELIST

By

Dr. Don Whitt

Title: *Doing the Work of the Evangelist*

Author: Dr. Don Whitt

Published by: Engedi Publishing LLC

Transcribed and Edited by: Marla J. Johnson

First Edition, January 2016

Published in the United States of America

Dedicated to the love of my life, Judith Ruth Whitt.
Gone from here, but present with the Lord.
November 22, 1949 – February 10, 2015

TABLE OF CONTENTS

FORWARD

The Lord has given special men to the church to reap a spiritual harvest. In the New Testament, they are called "evangelists." The Apostle Paul writes, *"And He gave some as apostles, and some as prophets, and SOME AS EVANGELISTS, and some as pastors and teachers, for the equipping of the saints for the work of service, to the building up of the body of Christ"* (Ephesians 4:11-12). To be sure, every pastor is to *"do the work of an evangelist"* (cf. 2 Timothy 4:5), and every Christian is to share the Gospel of Jesus with lost people in order to win them to salvation in Him (cf. Matthew 28:19-20; Acts 1:8; Romans 1:16). Nevertheless, God has blessed His church with men who have a special calling to not only "do the work of an evangelist," but to BE an evangelist twenty-four hours a day, every day of the year, for the rest of their lives!

Philip, one of the first deacons (Acts 6), became a full-time evangelist (Acts 21:8). The Bible says of Philip, *"Then Philip opened his mouth, and beginning from this Scripture he preached Jesus to him"* (Acts 8:35). That is what evangelists do, and that is what all of God's people should do when they engage in evangelism. We are to verbally share what the Bible says about Jesus to lost people! That is what Don Whitt does, day in and day out.

I have known Don for over three decades. I have preached in his churches when he was an evangelistic pastor,

5

and he has preached in mine. When he asked me to serve on his ministry's board, I immediately said, "Yes!" I believe in him. I pray for him and support his ministry financially. I know him to be a Godly man, a praying man, a church man, a family man, and above all, a soul-winning man. I love him. I preached at his wife's funeral. I know his three sons, all of whom love Jesus and have families that love Jesus. He is a man of God who has "done it right."

When I think of an "evangelist," three names immediately pop up in my mind – Billy Graham, Junior Hill, and Don Whitt. These are men who have given their lives to the winning of souls. They share Jesus one-on-one with lost people every day, not just when they are preaching from a pulpit.

In his new book, *Doing the Work of the Evangelist*, Don has set forth in print some of his greatest evangelistic sermons. These are sermons God has used to usher in thousands of precious souls to His kingdom. I have heard Don preach several of these sermons. A sermon is always better heard than read. However, like the sermons of Charles Spurgeon, when I read these sermons, I hear the voice of a prophet crying in the wilderness, "Prepare ye the way of the Lord! Make His paths straight!" I also hear the voice of our Savior, Jesus, saying, "Come unto Me all who are weary and heavy laden, and I will give you rest!"

This work will bless any Christian and any non-Christian. I plan to purchase copies of this book to give to other

Christians to build up their faith. I also plan to give copies to lost people so they can be saved.

We live in a culture that is growing more spiritually dark and decadent every day. It is a culture that needs to hear the old, old story of Jesus and His love. Thankfully, God still has a few faithful men who are "Doing the Work of an Evangelist"! Don Whitt is one of those men.

These words are not from the cold, removed study of an armchair theologian who rarely, if ever, engages lost people with the Gospel. Rather, these messages are straight from a red-hot pulpit, from the heart and lips of a man on fire for God! The same fire that burned in the prophet Jeremiah's heart burns in Don's. When you read these sermons, you will feel that Holy Ghost heat.

Read these sermons and be blessed. Share them with others, especially your lost loved ones. As you do, you too will be, "Doing the Work of the Evangelist"!

3 John 2,

Steve Gaines, Ph.D.
Senior Pastor
Bellevue Baptist Church
Memphis, TN

INTRODUCTION

The Apostle Paul exhorted us in II Timothy 4:5 to "do the work of an evangelist." In *Doing the Work of the Evangelist,* there are select sermons God gave me as I sought to fulfill the call of the evangelist on my life. I have preached these sermons over the last thirty years across the United States and around the world. Literally thousands of people responded to the call of God throughout that time.

Most sermon books are written to be published as a book. However, these sermons were transcribed from the recorded messages preached in church revivals and area-wide crusades. I trust you will catch a glimpse of the spirit, the excitement, the conviction, and the movement of God as they were being preached.

Although these are sermons God birthed and burned in my very soul, I do not claim any originality with them. My materials were gathered from many sources through the years. I am thankful for the pastors, evangelists, teachers, and friends who invested in me. Especially, I am thankful for these men from the past: J. Harold Smith, Adrian Rogers, and Stan Coffey. I am thankful for these men who are influencing my life now: Sam Cathey, James Merritt, Joe Arthur, and my pastor, Steve Gaines. So many of the stories and ideas come from them.

You may ask, "Why have you put these sermons in a book?" Here are the three main reasons:

1. Lost People Will Be Saved—If you are not a Christian, it is my prayer that as you read these messages, you will come to Christ in salvation.
2. Saved People Will Be Encouraged—Christian, I want you to be encouraged to do the work of the evangelist and to be a soul-winner for Christ.
3. Preachers Will Preach These Sermons—Preacher, you have my permission to use anything you find in this book as the Spirit of God makes it real in your life.

May you be blessed as you read *Doing the Work of the Evangelist.*

Don Whitt

CHAPTER 1

WHO IS THAT KNOCKING AT YOUR DOOR?

H ave you ever had someone knock on your door? Before you open up that door, you go over and you peep out the blinds. The reason you peep out those blinds is because you want to know who's knocking at your door. The reason you want to know who's knocking at that door is because you're going to make up your mind whether you're going to open up that door or not. Have you ever done that? I'm sure we've all done that. These days you better know who's knocking at that door before you open it.

Through the years there have been many times where I went around to knock on doors and I was not prepared for what was going to happen. Several years ago I was visiting one Saturday morning with one of my deacons. We were canvasing an apartment complex. I knocked on the door and this little high-pitched man's voice said, "Open the door and come on in." I never open the door. I want them to open the door for me. I looked over at the deacon to get instructions, and he looked back and said, "I don't know." So I knocked on the door again. The little high-pitched man's voice came back and said, "I said open the door and come on in." So again, I looked over at the deacon for instructions, and my deacon said, "Have at it, Preach." So, I opened up the door.

On the other side of that door was a little fellow—about 5-foot-3 or 5-foot-4—barefooted with cut-off blue jeans and a tee shirt on. He was squatting down and had a gun right in my face. I thought, "Oh Lord, this is the big one. I'm coming home." All of a sudden he went, "Bang, bang," and water went all over my face. I was not prepared for what happened when I knocked on that door!

In the Bible, there are three definite knocks. Each one of these knocks have a definite meaning for us.

1. THERE IS A KNOCK THAT IS NEVER IN VAIN.

Look over to Luke 11:9-10. Jesus said:

> *"And I say unto you, Ask, and it shall be given you; seek, and ye shall find; knock, and it shall be opened unto you. For every one that asketh receiveth; and he that seeketh findeth; and to him that knocketh it shall be opened."*

There is a knock that is never in vain. Jesus said there is a door and if any person at any time will come and knock on that door, that door will be opened. That simply means that any person who wants to be saved can be saved. As far as God is concerned, there is no reason for any person to walk out church doors lost without Christ. Jesus said, "Knock, and it shall be opened." We know that statement to be true for at least three reasons.

- **The word of God declares it.** No matter where you open the Bible, you're going to find the grace of God walking out to meet you. From Genesis to Revelation, the Spirit of God says, "Knock and it shall be opened."

- **The Son of God proclaims Himself to be that door.**
  Jesus said in John 10:9, *"I am the door: by Me if any man enter in, he shall be saved, and shall go in and out, and find pasture."* That simply means that if you come to Jesus, He'll save you.

- **The people of God can testify** that there was a time and a place where they knocked on that door and God opened that door and God saved their souls.

2. THERE IS A KNOCK THAT IS OFTEN IN VAIN.

In Revelation 3:20, Jesus is standing at the door and He said, *"Behold, I stand at the door, and knock: if any man hear My voice, and open the door, I will come in to him, and will sup with him, and he with Me."* There is a knock that is often in vain. There are three things I want you to notice about this knock.

- **Notice the Man who is knocking.** What you have here is a picture of Jesus. It's Jesus standing there and He's knocking. No doubt you have seen that beautiful painting by Holman Hunt where Christ is standing at the door. The first thing that jumps out to you when you look at that painting is this: there's no door handle on the outside of that door. That is a very important Scriptural truth. That lets you know God will never force His way into your life. Jesus will never kick in the door. If that door is going to be open, it must be opened from the inside. That's a very important Scriptural truth. Yet in that painting, the artist misrepresented something. He pictured Jesus there as a humble shepherd. If you look at the context, you're going to discover that the Jesus that's writing to those seven churches—and the Jesus that's standing at the door—is not a mansy-pansy, weak Jesus. Rather, He is God Almighty. He is the King of glory. He is King of Kings and the Lord of Lords. As Jesus comes and knocks at your heart's door, He's not knocking there as a humble shepherd but as God Almighty. That's the Man who is knocking.

- **Notice the methods He uses when He knocks.** When I search the Bible, I see there are two basic methods by which Jesus will come knocking.
  - ○ **He'll knock with blessings.** Romans 2:4 says:

    "Or despisest thou the riches of His goodness and forbearance and longsuffering; not knowing that the goodness of God leadeth thee to repentance?"

    God is a good God. You ought to get saved today. You ought to come to Christ today. You ought to get right with God today because of the goodness of God. That's the way God desires it to be. When God is blessing you, when God is being good to you, that's God saying, "I want to live in your heart." God says, "I put a roof over your head. I put clothes on your back. I put food on your table. I've given you a good husband, I've give you a good wife. I've given you good children, good friends, a good job. Please, let Me in." You see, when God is being good to you, that's God's way of saying, "I want to live in your heart." You say, "Preacher, God's good to everybody." That's right! God wants everybody to be saved! So often people misunderstand this. They think when everything's going good, when everything's going fine, that means they don't need God. Oh no, you've missed it. God is being good to you because God is saying, "I want to save you. I want to live in your heart." But if you do not open your heart's door when He knocks with blessings, then:

○ **He'll knock with burdens.** Look at Romans 2:8-9:

> *"But unto them that are contentious, and do not obey the truth, but obey unrighteousness, indignation and wrath, tribulation and anguish, upon every soul of man that doeth evil, of the Jew first, and also of the Gentile."*

If you do not open your heart's door when He comes knocking with blessings, then He'll come knocking with burdens. Have you ever heard someone give this kind of testimony? "I was in an automobile accident and as a result of that accident, I came to Christ." That was no accident. That was God's way of getting that person's attention, saying, "You need Me!" Some of you are going through family problems. That's God's way of saying, "You need Me!" Some of you are going through financial difficulties. That's God saying, "You need Me!" You find yourself in that hospital bed looking up at the face of God. That's God saying, "You need Me!" If you will not open your heart's door when He comes knocking with blessings, then He'll come knocking with burdens. Some of you, God has taken a 2x4 board and hit you over the head with it. You say, "I can't understand why I'm having all these problems." Bubba, wake up! That's God saying, "You need Me! Let Me save you!" Those are not just happen-chances. Rather, those are divine occurrences that God has allowed to come into your life so He can say, "You need Me! Let Me save you!"

- **Notice the missing of the knock.** Look back again at Revelation 3:20. Notice the verbs that are used in this passage. Jesus said, *"Behold, I stand at the door and knock: if any man hear My voice, and open the door, I will come in to him, and will sup with him, and he with me."* I'm not a Greek scholar, but I do know some things about the language and I know how to use certain tools. When I look at these verbs, they are very interesting. When you look at that verb, "Behold I stand," that's in the perfect-active tense. Then He says, "and knock," that's in the present-active tense. Aren't you impressed? Here's what that means: Jesus says, *"Behold I stand."*

15

He's taken His stand and it has everlasting and eternal and continual consequences. And then He said, *"and I knock."* And He knocks and He knocks and He knocks and He knocks.

Most of the time we don't understand that. We know He'll knock when we come to church. We know He'll knock when we have worship and music. We know He'll knock when the Bible is read. We know He'll knock when the preacher preaches. We know He'll knock when the invitation is extended. Somehow, we have the idea that when we walk out the church doors, He stops knocking. Yes, He will knock when the invitation is extended, but I want to tell you that when you walk out the doors after church, He's still knocking. When you get in that car, He's still knocking. When you go home, He's still knocking. When you go to school or to work, He's still knocking. You say, "Well, I just don't sense that." Let me explain it to you like this. When we're at church, we're focused on the Gospel. We've got our ears on. We're tuned in to God. When we leave church, there's so much noise out there. There's so much racket out there. We get in the car and we turn on the radio or put in a CD. We go home and turn on the TV. NASCAR starts up again—vrroooom! Braves lose again. Tennessee loses again. You don't care, but I do. We go to work or school and people are talking and laughing. Even still, Jesus has taken His stand and He's still knocking and knocking and knocking. He's going to keep on knocking until one of two things takes place—either you go to that door and open it and ask Him to come in, or the time may come when He stops knocking and He turns and walks away. Then you'll be able to go to church and not be troubled, not be bothered. You say, "Oh, everything's okay now." No! The worst of all things has happened! You've crossed over that deadline and He'll never knock again.

You know the most frightening thing about missing the knock? There are a lot of people who have the things of Jesus but they do not have Jesus. Years ago when I was in school out in Texas, I was pastoring a church in Mexia, Texas. There was an older couple there, May and Alvin Sellers. They sort of became our parents away from home. Brad was born out there and they became like his Papaw and Mamaw away from home. I'll never forget the first time we ate a meal at their home. When we finished eating, Mrs. Sellers looked at me and said, "Preacher, I'd like to show you Judy's room." Judy was their daughter who had died three years prior at 21 years of age. She just died suddenly. When I walked back in her room, I was not prepared for what I was going to see. There were all of her clothes hung up in her closet just like she left them. Over on her bed were all of her stuffed animals and dolls. On her nightstand and dresser were pictures of her when she was in middle and high school and college. Mrs. Sellers looked at me and said, "We left this

room like this because it just makes us feel like Judy is still here."
But Judy was not there. Oh, they had the things of Judy, but Judy
was not there.

You say, "I got baptized and it makes me feel like I have
Jesus. I give money to the church and it makes me feel like I
have Jesus. We have a big family Bible on our coffee table in
our home and it makes us feel like we have Jesus. We have a
picture on our wall of Jesus and it makes me feel like I have
Jesus." Just because you have the things of Jesus does not mean
you have Jesus. How do you get Jesus into your heart? When He
comes and He knocks, you go to that door and, through
repentance and faith, you open up that door and you ask Him to
come in. He'll come in and He'll save you.

3. THERE IS A KNOCK THAT IS ALWAYS IN VAIN.

Lost friend, there can come a time when it is too late to
be saved, too late to come to Christ, and too late to be forgiven.
Look over at Luke 13:22-25:

> *"And He went through the cities and villages,*
> *teaching, and journeying toward Jerusalem.*
> *Then said one unto Him, Lord, are there few that*
> *be saved? And He said unto them, strive to enter*
> *in at the strait gate: for many, I say unto you, will*
> *seek to enter in, and shall not be able. When once*
> *the master of the house is risen up, and hath shut*
> *to the door, and ye begin to stand without, and to*
> *knock at the door, saying, Lord, Lord, open unto*

us; and He shall answer and say unto you, I know
you not whence ye are. "

There is a knock that is always in vain. Jesus said there's going to come a day when some are going to come and knock on heaven's door. They're going to say, "Lord, did we not eat and drink in Your presence? Did I not preach in Your name? Did I not sing in Your name? Did I not teach in Your name? Did I not do this? Did I not do that in Your name?" The Lord is going to say, "Depart from Me, you work of iniquity. I never knew you." The Bible says the door is shut. When God shuts the door, you're a goner. When God shuts the door, there's no hope. How can the door be shut? Let me give you three ways.

- **The door can be shut by death.** When a person dies lost, there will be no more opportunities for them to be saved. You either get saved in this life or you'll never be saved. There are no second or third or fourth opportunities after death. There is no purgatory out there. You're either saved in this life or you'll never be saved. The truth of the matter is we don't know when we're going to die. One of my favorite philosophers is Yogi Berra, the Baseball Man. He had 10 World Series rings and he's in the Baseball Hall of Fame. Even more famous than being a baseball man, he was famous for his Yogisms. They're little statements he made. For example, he made the statement, "You'd better go to other people's funerals because they might not come to yours." Yogi said he'd ordered a pizza and he went to the pizza place to pick up the pizza. The pizza man said, "I've not cut up the pizza yet. Did you want that pizza cut up in 6 pieces or 12 pieces?" Yogi thought for a few moments, then said, "Well, you better cut it up in 6 pieces. I'm not real sure I can eat 12." Yogi also made the statement, "I know I'm going to die one day. I just don't want to be there when it happens." Well, Yogi, you were there. You couldn't get away from it. I can't get away from it. Every one of us has an appointment with Death if Jesus carries His coming. There have been people where Jesus knocked on their heart's door and they said, "No." They died and they're in hell now.

- **The door can be shut through the Second Coming of Jesus Christ.** Jesus is coming again. I believe His coming is very near. Jesus comes and He knocks on your heart's door but you say, "No." If Jesus were to come this afternoon, all we who are saved are going to be with Jesus! But if you're lost, you're going to be left behind, cast in the Great Tribulation, deceived by the Antichrist, and ultimately doomed to hell forever. You say, "Now wait a minute, Preacher. I remember reading a certain book or I remember seeing a certain video series that indicated many are going to be saved during the Tribulation period." I have a word for you: it won't be you. Second Thessalonians 2:10-11 says:

> *"Because they received not the love of the truth, that they might be saved. And for this cause God shall send them strong delusion, that they should believe a lie: that they might be damned."*

If you won't get saved in this place of love, if you won't get saved in this place of grace, you won't get saved when judgment begins to fall.

- **The door can be shut by you crossing over the deadline and sinning away your day of grace**. Let me illustrate it this way. Let's suppose I go out this afternoon and I knock on a door. They come over and peep out the blinds. They say, "There's the old preacher out there." They don't open the door. I think, "Apparently they're not dressed, or the house is a little messed up. Maybe they're embarrassed to have me come in right now. I'll just go on and make some more visits. I'll just come back in a while." Maybe an hour or two later, I knock on the same door again. Same thing happens. I think, "Apparently they just don't want me." I turn and walk away.

Some of you, ever since you were a little boy or a little girl, God's had His finger around your heart. He's been knocking and knocking and knocking. You've been saying, "No, no, no." Friend, you can say, "No," one time too many and cross over the deadline. You're just as sure of hell as if you were already there.

- ○ *"Wherefore God also gave them up to the uncleanness through the lusts of their own hearts."* – Romans 1:24
- ○ *"For this cause God gave them up unto vile affections."* – Romans 1:26
- ○ *"And even as they did not like to retain God in their knowledge, God gave them over to a reprobate mind."* – Romans 1:28

I believe there's somebody right now who will say "No," too many times. Maybe it's you. God will knock on your heart's door and you say, "No." You walk away from that moment and God signs your death warrant. The Holy Ghost will take His flight and never knock again. You say, "Preacher, whenever I get ready to get saved, I'll get saved." No, you won't! You'll only get saved if the Holy Ghost calls you! It's the only way you'll ever get saved. Genesis 6:3 says, *"My Spirit shall not always strive with man."* Sometimes I hear somebody say, "As long as there's life, there's hope." No! As long as the Holy Ghost is calling, there's hope.

I was preaching at a crusade in Mount Orab, Ohio. It was at a little fairground with a little preacher's stand in front of a set of bleachers. Every night there was an older gentleman who sat in a lawn chair at the bottom of the bleachers. On Friday night— the closing night of the crusade—the older gentleman came over to me. He looked at me and said, "Preacher, I took that step tonight." I said, "Good, great!" I thought he got saved. He looked back and said, "Oh no, Preacher. I took that step tonight. I crossed God's deadline and I'm going to hell."

You remember the first time Jesus knocked at your heart's door? I'm not talking about the first time you heard about Jesus. I'm talking about the first time He really knocked on your heart's door. The Spirit of God was calling. Remember how hard He was knocking? There's no doubt about it. He was knocking and saying, "I want to save you! Let Me come in! Let Me save you!" But you said, "No." The next time He knocked, it was not nearly as hard and not nearly as strong. But you said, "No." As you read this right now, you can barely hear Him knock. You better come while you can still hear Him knocking. A day may come when the Holy Ghost will take His flight and never knock again.

In my opinion, one of the greatest evangelists who has been in America over the last century was Dr. J. Harold Smith. There was no man who had a greater impact on my life personally and my family's life than Dr. J. Harold Smith. My mother got saved when she was 13 years old at a J. Harold Smith crusade at the old WNOX studio in Knoxville, Tennessee. Then I was raised most of my life by my grandparents on an old mountain farm in East Tennessee. We'd work in the fields in the morning then come in for dinner. My grandmother would always have the radio turned on, so I grew up listening to him preach. My grandmother even had a picture of him on the kitchen wall. I knew of J. Harold Smith my whole life.

When God called me to preach and I began to pastor, I always wanted him to come and preach revivals at the church I was pastoring. While I was pastor at First Baptist Church of Milan, Tennessee, he came twice to preach in revival meetings. Two of my three boys were saved at those revival meetings. We became very close friends. For the next twenty-plus years, I spent a lot of time with Dr. Smith, fellowshipping and traveling with him. When he passed away just a few years ago at the age of 91, I had the privilege to preach his funeral service. I say all that to say this: he was a man that was very close to me and had a great impact on my life.

I remember him telling about preaching a revival at First Baptist Church in Walhalla, South Carolina. Walhalla is just south of Greenville, South Carolina. It's right on the edge of the Georgia-South Carolina line. He said that one night the power of God moved in the church in a very real and very powerful way. When he gave the invitation, the altar and the aisle filled with people being saved. But some way, somehow, he still sensed that someone was getting their last call, their last opportunity they'd ever have to get saved. It's a weighty experience for a pastor to come to an invitation and sense that someone there has a last chance. Dr. Smith looked up and on the back row was a father, mother, and teenage daughter. He said he could not get to them because the altar and aisles were so full of people. He had to get to them, though. So he stood on the front pew and walked from pew to pew to get to the back of the church.

When he got back there, he looked at the father and asked, "Sir, are you a Christian?" "Yes." Then he looked at the mother and asked, "Ma'am, are you a Christian?" "Yes." Then he looked at the teenage daughter and asked, "Sweetheart, what's your name?" "Katie."

"How old are you, Katie?"

"Fourteen."

"Katie, are you a Christian?"

"No."

"Katie, won't you let me lead you in a prayer and you ask Jesus to save you?"

"No!"

"Katie, if you knew you were to die tonight, wouldn't you let me lead you in a prayer and you ask Jesus to save you?"

She looked back and she said, "Preacher, if I knew I'd be dead by midnight, I wouldn't let you pray for me."

Dr. Smith said he turned and made his way back down to the front, rejoiced in all the decisions that had been made, and dismissed the congregation. Katie and her parents walked out and got in their car. They drove down the highway, pulled into a service station, filled their tank full of gas, continued down the highway, then turned right onto Highway 183. They lived about three miles down that road on the left. There was a car approaching them, so they stopped in front of their driveway and turned on the left turn signal. Katie and her parents didn't know that in the other car were three drunk men driving over 90 miles an hour. As they waited, the other car got closer and closer to them. It ran head-on into their car, knocking their car 40-50 yards down the highway. The drunks' car rolled another 20-30 yards. All three drunk men crawled out of their car—not a scratch, not a bruise. The mother and father got out of their car— miraculously, not a scratch, not a bruise. But little Katie was wedged in the back seat and could not get out.

Just then, another car pulled up to the scene. Two men jumped out. They saw what happened and ran toward Katie to try to get her out of the seat. She was wedged in so tight they could not get her out. All the while, the gas overflowed from the full tank and made its way down the highway where the drunks stood in a stupor. One of the drunk men reached into his right pocket and pulled out a cigarette. Then he reached into his left pocket and pulled out a box of matches. He lit the match, lit the cigarette, and threw the match on the highway where it hit the gas. Flames instantly burst off the ground, then quickly made their way back up the gas trail and engulfed the car. The two men, realizing they too were going to perish in the flames, had to back out. The mother was getting ready to jump into the flames to rescue her little girl. She pushed against the men as they restrained her. She cried out, "Katie, Katie! We can't get you out of the car! Katie, call on Jesus and He'll save you!" They said the last thing they heard before the car exploded into flames was that little girl saying, "I wish I'd let Preacher Smith pray for me."

I know what some of you are thinking. You're thinking, "A preacher ought not tell stories like this. You're trying to scare people." I wish I could! I'd rather scare you into heaven than lull you into hell. I'm trying to get you to realize that you can say "No" to Jesus right now and you can be in hell by this time tomorrow. Lost friend, do you hear Jesus knocking on your heart's door? Do you hear Him knocking? Do you hear that knock? What are you going to do? Won't you go to that door and, through repentance and faith, open up that door and ask Him to come in? He'll come in and He'll save you.

CHAPTER 2

PERSUADED

W e're going to begin in Romans 4:20-21. The Bible says:

> *"He* [that is, Abraham] *staggered not at the promise of God through unbelief; but was strong in faith, giving glory to God; And being fully persuaded* [underline that word *fully* in your Bible] *that what He had promised, He was able also to perform."*

Then look back at Luke 16:30-31. This is the story of the rich man and Lazarus. The rich man died and went hell, but Lazarus went to heaven. Notice in verse 30-31 that the rich man is in hell.

> *"And he said, Nay, father Abraham: but if one went unto them from the dead, they will repent. And he said unto him, If they hear not Moses and the prophets, neither will they be persuaded* [underline that word *neither*], *though one rose from the dead."*

Now let's look at Acts 26:28. Paul preached the Gospel to King Agrippa and in verse 28 Agrippa is responding. *"Then Agrippa said unto Paul, Almost thou persuadest me to be a Christian."* Underline there in your Bible the word *almost*.

I'm preaching on the subject of being "Persuaded: Fully, Never, and Almost."

We live in a day of uncertainty. Old timers would have to admit that there's never been a day like the days in which we're living. I know we've said that through the years. Still, anyone over 40 years of age will have to admit that there's never been a time like we're living in today. The Bible says in Proverbs 27:1, *"Boast not thyself of to morrow; for thou knowest not what a day may bring forth."*

Over a year ago, I had that statement hit me right between the eyes like never before. My normal schedule is to leave on Saturday and to either drive or fly to where I'm going to go preach. Normally, I come back home on Thursday. That Thursday I came back home a little after noon. My wife met me in the kitchen. She said, "I have a little numbness here in my cheek and I have a little numbness in the ends of my fingers." With her being a nurse, she already figured out what was wrong with her. She said, "I believe I've got Bell's palsy or perhaps I've had a light stroke. I don't know, but I've got an appointment with the doctor this afternoon."

She went on to the doctor in Jackson, Tennessee where we live. The doctor ran a CAT scan. Then he said, "I really believe we need to do an MRI in the morning." So, Friday morning she went back in to run the MRI, then came home. It was about 2 in the afternoon when the doctor's office called and said, "You need to get back down here really quick." Whenever you get a call like that from the doctor's office, you know it's not good news. She made her way back down to the doctor's office. He said, "You have a tumor here in the front side of your brain; it's the size of a golf ball. We've already got you set up to see a neurosurgeon in Jackson next week." Judy said, "No, I'd really rather not see a neurosurgeon here. I'd rather go to M.D. Anderson out in Houston." He said, "Well, you'll never get to see a doctor out there." She replied, "I'm going to try."

On Monday morning, she called M. D. Anderson. She told them what was going on and that she needed to see a doctor. On Tuesday morning, she called back and asked, "When's my appointment?" They said, "This coming Friday at 8 o' clock." I was in revival that week in West Tennessee, traveling back and forth nightly. On Wednesday night when the revival was over, we drove toward Houston. We drove all the way through Thursday and got there Thursday night. On Friday morning, we met with the neurosurgeon. He'd already looked through the tests that had been run in Jackson. He said, "You have a Glioblastoma, Stage IV, here in the front side of your brain. We have set up surgery for you next Thursday at 8 o' clock." We had not planned on staying out there. We didn't take enough clothes to stay, but we just did what we had to do. We stayed through the weekend; Monday through Wednesday, they ran all other kinds of tests on her. On Thursday, they performed the surgery. The doctor came out and said the surgery was very successful. They removed over 98% of the tumor. We stayed out there for two weeks. When that was over, we drove back home and had a little period of waiting. Then she went under the watch care of M.D. Anderson, but took chemotherapy and radiation treatments in Memphis for the next six weeks.

The day after she completed her chemo and radiation, her colon perforated. We had to rush her to the hospital. She bottomed out twice even on the way to the hospital. They performed emergency surgery on her all through the night. For the next six weeks, she was in the intensive care unit on a ventilator. For the next seven months after she went in with the colon perforation, she was never able to come home. Then, she passed away. I miss her, but I'll see her again.

That one day when I walked in there and she said, "I have a little numbness in my cheek and in my fingers," my life completely changed. *"Thou knowest not what one day may bring forth."* If you don't know what one day will bring forth, how do you know what's going to be out there in your life? How do you know what's going to take place next week? Or next month? Or next year? *"Thou knowest not what a day may bring forth."*

Not only is there uncertainty in what one day may bring forth, there's also uncertainty in our nation today. Our nation is in a mess. What's taking place in our nation I believe may well determine whether we survive as a nation. I was reading a book sometime back by one of the big prophecy writers. He said that God doesn't care at all about America because there is no mention of America in the prophecies. I don't know about all that, but I do know this much: God loves souls. God loves sinners. God will save anyone who will trust Christ. God will bless any nation who will bless Israel. God will bless any nation who has churches who will send missionaries around the world to preach the Gospel. I believe that God wants to send revival to America.

There's also uncertainty in our economy. If you're not concerned about your money, you're different from most people I know. Most likely you're lying about it, too. The economy will be up one day then down the next. One day you have a dollar in your pocket; the next day it'll be empty. One day you'll be driving down the highway and you'll see the gas prices drop down to where you think it ought to be. Then the next day you drive by again and they shot back up. Someone in the Middle East sneezed. There's an uncertainty in our economy.

There's a spirit of uncertainty in the family. The very definition of marriage is being redefined by some. Just a few months ago the Presbyterian USA Church said they are now recognizing same-sex marriages. Even a First Baptist Church in South Carolina said they are going to recognize same-sex marriages. You don't find that in the Word of God.

While I'm in the neighborhood and I'm driving down the street, let me say this: marriage is between a man and a woman. Two men living together, or two women living together, is a sin and an abomination against Holy God. I don't care what Obama says; I don't care what Congress says; I don't care what the Supreme Court says. It's sin. I thank God the Supreme Court does not have the final word on it. They're not the final judge. I like what Dr. Adrian Rogers, who was the pastor at Belleview, used to say: "the Supreme Court has two brains. One went out to lunch and the other went to look for it."

There is a spirit of uncertainty in the world today. We may not know what one day might bring forth. We may not know what the future is for our nation, our economy, or our families. But there are some things we can know with certainty. We can know that God is real. We can know that we're saved. We can know that we're going to heaven one day when we die.

I want us to look at that word *persuade*. It literally means "to be thoroughly convinced." It means to be absolutely assured and to be won over by a powerful argument. Aren't you glad that when you were a lost sinner, you heard a man of God stand up and preach the Word of God and you believed? You trusted. You were thoroughly convinced. You were persuaded, and God saved your soul.

I want us to look at that word *persuade* around these 3 things: fully, never, and almost.

1. **FULLY.**

In Romans 4, Paul looked back thousands of years ago and used Abraham as an example. Abraham was 100 years old and his wife, Sarah, was 90 years old. Now, I don't want to discourage anyone, but when you're 100, and your wife is 90, it's a pretty good indication that you're not going to have any more babies at your house. I'm not near 100, and if anything like that happened over at my house, buddy, it would be, "Elizabeth, this is the big one. I'm coming home!" God told Abraham and Sarah that they were going to have a son named Isaac. No one believed God other than Abraham. The Bible says in Romans 4:21, *"and being fully persuaded that, what He had promised, He was able also to perform."* Paul said that if Abraham staggered not at the promise of God, that if Abraham could be fully persuaded in regards to the promise of that earthly Isaac, how much more should we be persuaded in regards to that heavenly Isaac, the Lord Jesus Christ. If Abraham, without a Gospel preacher, could believe God, then how much more should we believe God today?

Apparently, the word *persuade* began to bubble up in the heart and the mind of Paul. Paul picks up with that word again in II Timothy 1:12:

> *"For the which cause I also suffer these things: nevertheless I am not ashamed: for I know whom I have believed and am persuaded that He is able to keep that which I have committed unto Him against that day."*

I love that word, *know.* In the Bible there are 2 words used for the word *know*:

- There is a knowledge we gain by experience.
- There is a knowledge we gain because we know God.

There are some things I know from experience. I know that fire burns. I know that snakes are dangerous. I hate snakes. I don't care what kind of snakes they are, I hate snakes. I don't care if they are black snakes, spotted snakes, or green snakes. I hate snakes. I don't care if they are little snakes or big snakes. I hate snakes. I don't even care if they are live snakes or dead snakes. I hate snakes! I made that statement a while back and after the service a woman came up and showed me a picture. She said, "I want to show you a picture of my pet snake." She had a big ol' snake wrapped around her neck. I said, "That's stupid." I know that's not a good word to use, but that's what it is. That's stupid! I hate snakes! I know that bee stings hurt. I know that most men don't know anything about women. There are just some things we know by experience.

Then there is a knowledge we gain by knowing God. There's a knowledge—an assurance, a confidence—that God puts in you and imparts in you when He saves your soul. I don't know I'm saved just because of experience; although, we do experience God when we're saved. I know I'm saved because I know God. There's a knowledge that we have that the world does not have. You say, "Does that make us better than the world?" Not necessarily, but I am glad that in a world of uncertainties, I know God. The Bible says here, *"For I know whom I have believed."* Salvation is not in the church, in baptism, in the Lord's supper, or in religious activity. Salvation is not in a plan, but in a Person, and His name is Jesus. For I know whom I have believed.

Someone came to me one time and said, "Preacher, you're preaching an easy believism." I said, "What do you mean?" He replied, "You stand up there and say that if a person will come to Jesus, if they'll trust Jesus, if they'll believe in Jesus, then God will save them." I said, "Well, I'm glad you listened! I preach that because that's what the Bible preaches."

- *"Sirs, what must I do to be saved? And they said, Believe on the Lord Jesus Christ, and thou shalt be saved."* – Acts 16:30-31

- *"He that believeth on the Son hath everlasting life."* – John 3:36

- *"That if thou shalt confess with thy mouth the Lord Jesus, and believe in thine heart that God hath raised Him from the dead, thou shalt be saved. For with the heart man believeth unto righteousness; and with the mouth confession is made unto salvation. For the Scripture saith, Whosoever believeth on Him shall not be ashamed."* – Romans 10:9-11

You can know without a doubt that you're saved. Paul said, *"I know whom I have believed and am persuaded."* There's that word. You couldn't talk Paul out of his salvation. You couldn't talk Paul into following another Jesus or following another gospel. He said, *"I know whom I have believed and am persuaded."* You say, "Preacher, aren't you afraid that some false preacher might come along and lead you astray?" Listen, when God saved me as a 13-year-old boy at Blue Springs Baptist Church in Rutledge, Tennessee in 1963, God put the Holy Ghost in me. Ever since that moment, whenever I hear a false teacher or false prophet, there's something in me that raises up and says, "Liar! Liar! Liar! I know whom I have believed and am persuaded that He is able!" Listen: God is able! I don't care who you are today, God is able to save you! You may come here today and think, "There's no hope for me." I don't care who you are or how much in the grips of sin you are, God is able to set you free. You may be bound by alcohol or drugs, but God is able to set you free. Your marriage and family may be falling apart, but God is able to put it back together. God is able! Thank God He is able to keep that which I've committed to Him against that day.

I have a secret ministry I don't normally let people in on. I've got two preacher boys and a lawyer and they say, "Daddy, what you do is coo-coo." Well, I'll just keep on being coo-coo. I have an elevator ministry. When I get on an elevator and the door shuts, I start preaching. They can't run. They can't get away. When Judy and I were out in Houston, the hospital was way up high, about 20-25 stories up. One day, we got on that elevator and were standing in the back. I waited until it packed full and the door shut; I had them. I began to preach, "Sure is great to be saved! Sure is great to know Jesus! I'm a winner! I can't lose! If this thing goes up, I go up. If this thing goes down, I still go up! I can't lose!" There was a wiry looking guy standing near the front. He was wearing cut-off jeans with little wiry legs. He looked back at me and said, "I believe I might come back as a blue bird. Or I might come back as a robin." I said, "You probably will!" You say, "Well, I just don't believe that a person can really know that they know that they know that they're saved." Then you don't believe the Bible. The Bible does not preach or teach a think so, maybe so, hope so, reckon so salvation. But this Bible does preach a know so, life changing, certain salvation. You're able to lay your head on the pillow at night and say, "Blessed assurance, Jesus is mine! Oh, what a foretaste of glory divine!"

Paul's not finished yet. He picks up with this word over in Romans 8. I cannot turn to Romans 8 without turning to verse 28 because this verse has become so real to me over the last year. *"And we know that all things work together for good to them that love God, to them who are called according to His purpose."* Then verse 33. *"Who shall lay any thing to the charge of God's elect? It is God that justifieth."* No one can bring your sin up against you. The devil can't. God won't—they're gone! Look over to verse 35. *"Who shall separate us from the love of Christ? Shall tribulation, or distress, or persecution, or famine, or nakedness, or peril, or sword?"* Nothing shall separate us from the love of Christ!

Then look over to verse 37. *"Nay, in all these things we are more than conquerors through Him that loved us."* I love that phrase, *more than*. Not just joy, but joy unspeakable and full of glory! Not just life, but abundant, eternal, and everlasting life! Not just peace, but peace that passes all understanding! Not just a cup full, but my cup runneth over! More than conquerors through Him who loves us! Verse 38 continues:

"For I am persuaded, that in neither death, nor life, nor angels, nor principalities, nor powers, now things present, nor things to come, nor height, nor depth, nor any other creature, shall be able to separate us from the love of God, which is in Christ Jesus our Lord."

You can be fully persuaded that you're saved and you're going to stay saved! Is there anything better than being saved? Yes! It's being saved and knowing it! Is there anything better than being saved and knowing it? Yes! It's being saved and knowing it and knowing you're going to stay saved!

Are you saved? Do you know that you're saved? Are you fully persuaded that you're saved? If I did not know that I was saved, if I did not know that when I died I was going to be with God in heaven, there is no way that I would do anything else without settling it once and for all!

2. NEVER.

Look on over now to Luke 16:27. I want you to see that word *never*. As was mentioned, this is the story of the rich man and Lazarus. The rich man is crying out from hell.

"I pray thee therefore, father, that thou wouldest send him to my father's house: For I have five brethren; that he may testify unto them, lest they also come into this place of torment. Abraham

saith unto him, They have Moses and the prophets; let them hear them. And he said, Nay, father Abraham: but if one went unto them from the dead, they will repent. And he said unto him, If they hear not Moses and the prophets, neither will they be persuaded though one rose from the dead."

Here was this man in hell and he begins to think of his five lost brothers. By the way, when a person gets saved, they want everyone else to get saved. When a lost person dies and goes to hell, they don't want anyone else to go with them. He says, "Raise someone up from the dead! Send them to my five brothers so they won't follow me to this place of torment!" But in essence, God says, "That's impossible. If they will not hear Moses and the prophets, neither will they be persuaded though one rose from the dead." You know what that means? That means if you won't get saved right now by the clear preaching from the Bible, you wouldn't get saved if God were to raise someone from the dead.

Let's suppose we go out to the cemetery. I'll be honest with you; that's not where I want to spend most of my time. Still, I walk over to the tombstone of a very prominent person who lived in the community 50 years ago. I go knock on that tombstone and say, "Dead man! Come out of that grave!" That grave begins to burst open. All of a sudden, Mr. Skeleton pops out. I look at him and say, "Mr. Skeleton, I'm preaching over at the church. I just can't get some of those folks to listen. I believe if you were to go over and give your testimony, some of them might get saved. Would you be willing to do that?" He says, "Well, yeah!" So, I get a black tuxedo and wrap it around him and put a hat on top of that ol' bald, skully head. I put him in my truck and we make our way to the front of the church. Word starts getting around, "Man's been dead for 50 years! Been in hell for 50 years! Going to give his testimony tonight!" You wouldn't be able to fit them all in the building. Every television station in Atlanta, Chattanooga, Birmingham would be there. We walk in to the building, make our way to the front of the stage. Mr. Skeleton rattles to the front row and sits down. I stand up and say, "Ladies and gentlemen, we have something very unusual today. We've got a man who's been dead and in hell for 50 years. He's going to give his testimony. Let's welcome him." He rattles over to the pulpit and says, "Now folks, I've been dead for 50 years. I've been in hell for 50 years! Don't follow me. Get saved." He rattles back over and sits down. I stand up again and say, "Folks, you heard Mr. Skeleton. We're going to stand and I'm going to ask you to come and get saved." According to Jesus, how many people would be saved? Zero. *"If they will not hear Moses and the prophets, neither will they be persuaded though one rose from the dead."* That means if you will not get saved by the clear preaching like I'm doing right now, you wouldn't get saved if God were to write your name in the sky.

You say, "Preacher, are you saying there are some people who will never get saved?" That's exactly right. Don't misunderstand me. This Bible preaches a "Whosoever will" Gospel. If you want to be saved, you can be saved. It's not that they cannot be saved, but they refuse to be saved! I stand at the pulpit and I preach the Gospel. I preach that Christ died on the cross for you. I preach that Christ was placed in that tomb. I preach that three days later Jesus came out of that grave and He's alive. I preach to you that Christ loves you. I preach that Christ wants to save you. I preach that God wants you to spend an eternity with Him in heaven. The choice is yours now. You have to make the choice. Every Christian had to make the choice to be saved. No one forced them to be saved! I'm going to ask you, make the right choice. If I had the least inkling whatsoever, if I sensed at all that the Spirit of God was calling me, I would not wait to get it settled. I'd fall on my face now, I'd be crying out now, "My God, in the name of Jesus I repent of my sins! Jesus, come in to my heart and save my soul."

3. ALMOST.

Paul preached the Gospel to King Agrippa in Acts 26. In verse 26, Paul says:

> *"For the king knoweth of these things, before whom I also speak freely: for I am persuaded that none of these things are hidden from him; for this thing was not done in a corner. King Agrippa, believest thou the prophets? I know that thou*

believest. Then Agrippa said unto Paul, Almost thou persuaded me to be a Christian."

Wouldn't you have loved to hear that sermon? Wouldn't you have loved to be a fly on the wall there and hear Paul preach?? Paul was a powerful preacher, a powerful persuader because he'd been persuaded himself.

There ain't nothing like hearing a man preach about being saved who's saved himself. There's nothing like hearing a man preach about the blood of Jesus who's been washed in the blood of Jesus himself. I know I may not be the best preacher. I stomp. I shout. I spit and splutter sometimes. But let me tell you: I believe every bit of it. I know I'm saved. I know Christ lives in my heart. I know I'm going to heaven one day when I die. Let me tell you, it's real! It's real to me!

Paul was persuaded and he preached a powerful persuasive message. You can almost see King Agrippa. His heart begins to melt. His hands begin to tremble. His chin begins to quiver. He's about ready to reach out and take Paul by the hand, but jerks it back. He begins to think, "If I trust this Christ, what's it going to cost me in my political career?" He looks back at Paul and in essence, he says, "Paul, you're good at what you do. Almost you persuaded me to be a Christian."

What are the results of being almost persuaded? Let me give you 3 results.

- **To be almost persuaded is to be lost altogether.** It does not count to be close. Some of you one day are going to

43

stand before God and say, "Lord, Lord! I went to church." That's almost, but not enough. "Lord, Lord, I got baptized." That's almost, but not enough. "Lord, Lord. I lived a good life." That's almost, but not enough.

- **To be almost persuaded hinders other people.** If Agrippa had been saved, could it be that Bernice, Felix, and Festus would have been saved, too? Could it be that the entire nation could have been moved toward Christ? What about that little boy who's following in your footsteps? Where are you taking him? What about that little daughter who loves you so much and takes every step that you take? Where are you taking her?

- **To be almost persuaded is to die and go to hell.** That's the worst thing of all about being almost persuaded. King Agrippa died and went to hell himself. I don't read any place in the Bible where Agrippa got saved. I don't read anything in the Bible where Agrippa ever called on Christ for salvation. Here's the saddest thing about it: God loved Agrippa just like He loved Paul. Jesus died for Agrippa just like He died for Paul. God gave Agrippa every opportunity to be saved just like He gave Paul and just like He's giving every one of you.

In my opinion, one of the greatest evangelists who have been in America over this past century was Dr. J. Herald Smith. He had more influence upon my life and my family's life than any other preacher I know. I became very close friends with him.

44

When he passed away a few years ago at the age of 91, I had the privilege, along with Dr. James Merritt, to preach at his funeral service. For over 20 years, I spent a lot of time with J. Herald Smith, just gleaning from him and hearing him talk about his experiences out of his ministry.

He told the story about preaching a tent crusade in Greenville, South Carolina. One night when he was preaching, there were four teenagers sitting on the back row—two boys and two girls—and they were mocking him. They were mimicking him as he preached. If you ever saw J. Herald Smith preach, he was very animated. I am calm compared to J. Herald Smith. He'd run, kick his leg, wave his arm. When he waved his arm, they'd wave their arms back at him. When he made a point, they laughed and mocked him while he was preaching. When it had gotten to the invitation, he pleaded with them to think seriously about what they were doing and to come to Christ, but they refused.

As he was standing at the back of the tent and greeting people as they left, the four teenagers came by him. He took one of the boys by the hand and held it. He looked at him and said, "Young man, you didn't mock me tonight, but you mocked God. Even still, God loves you and God wants to save you. Trust Christ." That young boy looked back at him and said, "Old man, I don't have time for you. Me and my buddy are going to take these two girls out tonight. We're going to drink beer. We're going to have sex with them. We don't have time for that." It was like he just shoved God and Jesus and the Bible and the Holy Ghost in to the face of the man of God. They walked on out to their car and drove off.

Dr. Smith said he and the pastor stood there for about 10 more minutes. An ambulance drove by with the siren on. Then a police car drove by with the siren on. He said, "Pastor, let's go see what's happening." They got in their car and drove down the road about half a mile. There was a curve there in the road. On the other side of that curve there was a car that was in flames. It had run off the road, hit a big tree, and exploded. It was the car with those four teenagers in it.

Go back with me in your mind half a mile. Go back with me in your mind ten minutes earlier. What if those teenagers, instead of turning and going out, had turned and walked down the aisle to an old fashioned altar and got on their faces and cried out to God for salvation? Then, if they had gotten in that wreck, instead of going to hell, they would have gone to heaven. You see, it's just that close. You have the choice to make. Am I going to turn and go away or am I going to turn and come to Christ? Sir, you can make that choice. Ma'am, you can make that choice. You can either turn and go away or you can turn and come to Christ. That's just how close it is. One day you'll hear the last sermon you'll ever hear. Don't turn and walk away. Turn to Christ. Come to Jesus. He'll save you.

CHAPTER 3

HOW TO WIN YOUR FAMILY TO CHRIST

I suppose the greatest desire of any Christian is to see their family members come to Christ. Now, we want to see anyone saved. But especially we want to see our family members being saved. I want to talk about a very practical way to win your family to Christ.

I'm reading for our beginning text from the Esther 8:6. Esther cries out and says, *"For how can I endure to see the evil that shall come to my people? Or how can I endure to see the destruction of my kindred?"*

The book of Esther is a strange part of the Word of God. I say that because the name of God is not found one time in the entire book of Esther. But although the name of God is not found, there is a love and a compassion and a tenderness that it must come from God. Also, the love and the judgment and the providential dealings of God are woven throughout the book.

The story of Esther is very thrilling and very moving. Really, if you were going to make a movie, the story of Esther and all that takes place in this book would make an exciting movie. It's a story of a Jewish maiden who, in the providence of God, was elevated to a place of great influence and great power. God used her to literally change the course of history for 127 provinces. She had more power than a heathen king and a wicked prime minister put together.

In this passage we hear Esther cry out and say, *"How I can endure to see the destruction of my kindred?"* In order to understand why Esther is making that plea, you must look back just a few pages to Esther 3:13. The Bible says:

> *"And the letters were sent by post into all the king's provinces, to destroy, to kill, and to cause to perish, all Jews, both young and old, little children and women."*

Through the evil maneuvering of the wicked prime minister Haman, a decree has been sent out to kill and destroy all of Esther's people, both women and children, young and old. They were all put under the sentence of death by the hand of this wicked one. Esther was so moved by this that she determined in her heart and cried out and said, *"How can I endure to see the destruction of my kindred?"* So, she determines no matter what, she is going to save her people.

You and I need to understand that our unsaved loved ones—our unsaved mothers and fathers, sons and daughters, brothers and sisters—have been placed under the sentence of death at the hand of the wicked one because of sin.
The Bible says:

- *"Be sure your sin will find you out."* – Ezekiel 18:20
- *"For the wages of sin is death."* – Romans 6:23
- *"Wherefore, as by one man sin entered into the world, and death by sin; and so death passed upon all men, for*

that all have sinned." – Romans 5:12

Our unsaved loved ones have been placed under the sentence of death and we must do something. We must be like Esther. We must get desperate. We must get determined that we're going to win our loved ones no matter the cost. I believe the saddest hour of a Christian is to stand over an open grave of an unsaved loved one. I hope you never have to know in your heart that your loved one is in hell forever and ever.

As I look through the Bible, I'm amazed by how much God emphasized that it's His desire and His heartbeat to see the entire family be saved. In Acts 16, Paul and Silas had been preaching the Gospel. As a result, they had been arrested, beaten, and placed in prison. The Bible says that it was midnight. They were praying and praising God. Now, that is one good indication that they were not Baptist. If they were Baptist, they would have been complaining about how the pastor hadn't come by to see them yet. At midnight, God shook that prison to such a degree that the doors flew open. The jailor, thinking the prisoners had escaped, fell before Paul and Silas. The Bible says he was trembling and he cried out and said, *"Sirs, what must I do to be saved?"* They said, *"Believe on the Lord Jesus Christ and thou shalt be saved, and thine house."*

In Genesis 7, God gave Noah instructions to build the ark. The judgment flood was coming. Then God spoke to Noah, and He said, *"Come into the ark."* By the way, God didn't say, "Go into the ark." He said, "Come into the ark." You know what that means to me? God was in the ark. He said *"Come into the ark and thine house with thee."* Don't ever think a man does a bad job and don't ever call a man a failure if he gets his family in the ark. Noah got his family into the ark.

Then in Joshua 24, Joshua, that great general, cried out and said, *"Choose this day whom you will serve, but as for me and my house, we will serve the Lord."* Throughout the Word of God, you're going to find that God emphasizes it's His will and His desire to see our families come to Christ.

Catherine Booth, who was the wife of William Booth, the founder of the Salvation Army, prayed this prayer. She said, "Oh God, I will not stand before Thee unless all my children come with me." Now, how many of you mothers have prayed that way? How many of you fathers have that kind of fortitude? Did you know that every one of Catherine Booth's sons were saved and became preachers of the Gospel? I'm convinced that happened as a result that they had a mother who said, "God, I'm not going to stand before Thee unless all my children come with me."

When we get to that point in our lives, then we'll begin to see our loved ones being won to Christ. With that in way of introduction, I want you to see three main things.

1. THE CONDITION OF OUR UNSAVED LOVED ONES.

Most likely, you'll never do a great deal in leading your unsaved loved ones to Christ unless you are gripped with their spiritual condition. We must see them as they really are. We must not let our love for them or their love for us or their kindness for us blind us to their true spiritual condition. We must see them as lost, undone, unclean, and hell-bound. Only then will we be motivated to do anything in regards to winning them to Jesus. Let me just share with you a few things about what the Bible says about the spiritual condition of our unsaved loved ones.

- **Our unsaved loved ones are lost.** The Bible says:
  - *"The Son of Man has come to seek and to save that which was lost."* – Luke 19:10
  - *"For if our Gospel be hid, it is hid to them that are lost."* – 2 Corinthians 4:3

  I am convinced that the saddest word in the human language is the word *lost*. Think of what it means to be lost. Lost to God. Lost to Jesus. Lost to heaven. Lost to the church. Lost to the family. To be lost. If we could only see the agony and the pain that is wrapped up in the word *lost*, your church would be thrust into the greatest revival it has ever experienced. If we could only understand that our unsaved loved ones are lost. They're lost.

- **Our unsaved loved ones are condemned.** The Bible says:
  - *"He that believeth on Him is not condemned: but he that believeth not is condemned already."* – John 3:18

Our unsaved loved ones are condemned—condemned to eternal separation and damnation from God.

- **Our unsaved loved ones are spiritually blind.** The Bible says:

  ○ *"But if our gospel be hid, it is hid to them that are lost: in whom the god of this world hath blinded the minds of them which believe not, lest the light of the glorious gospel of Christ, who is the image of God, should shine unto them."* – 2 Corinthians 4:3-4

  ○ *"Let them alone: they be blind leaders of the blind. And if the blind lead the blind, both shall fall into the ditch."* – Matthew 15:14

Many of you have loved ones that are blind. Many of them are sitting under blind teachers and preachers. They need to be saved from that false religion to a saving knowledge of Jesus. They're blind!

By the way, have you ever been in a real, red-hot revival? Have you ever been in a real, red-hot revival where God is moving and people are being saved? You can almost reach out and touch God. Have you ever had that experience? You can almost feel God there in the midst. Maybe you walk outside and you have a family member who's not saved. They look over at you and say, "I just don't see it. I just don't see it the way you do. I don't understand it the way you do." Hey listen: they don't. They don't. That is the condition of an unsaved loved one. They're spiritually blind.

- **Our unsaved loved ones are without hope.** The Bible says:

- ○ *"That at that time ye were without Christ, being aliens from the commonwealth of Israel, and strangers from the covenants of promise, having no hope, and without God in the world."* – Ephesians 2:12

Some of you have mothers and fathers, or you have sons and daughters who have all the things of the world, but they have no hope.

- **Our unsaved loved ones are spiritually dead.** The Bible says:
  - ○ *"And you hath he quickened, who were dead in trespasses and sins."* – Ephesians 2:1

Some of you are living in the home of the walking, talking, living dead. They're dead to God. They're dead to Christ. They're dead to heaven. They're dead.

- **Our unsaved loved ones are counting on us.** So often we wait too late to ever try to win them to Jesus. Remember in Luke 16 about the rich man who died and went to hell? When he got to hell, he got concerned about his five brothers and wanted someone to go witness to them. It was too late!

2. THE CONCERN WE MUST HAVE FOR OUR UNSAVED LOVED ONES.

Most likely, unless there is a concern on our part to win them to Jesus, they'll never be saved. I thank God, in days gone by, there have been those who knew what it meant to have a concern and a burden for people to be saved. The Apostle Paul knew what it meant to have a concern to see people saved. He said in Romans 9:1-3:

> *"I say the truth in Christ, I lie not, my conscience also bearing me witness in the Holy Ghost, that I have great heaviness and continual sorrow in my heart. For I could wish that myself were accursed from Christ for my brethren, my kinsmen according to the flesh."*

That word *accursed* there means to be severed, to be cut off. In essence, he is saying, "I'd be willing to die and go to hell in order that my fellow Jews would be saved!" There is a great deal of difference between what I read there and what I see in most of our churches today. It's hard enough to get people to be faithful on Sunday morning, Sunday night and Wednesday night, much less to have a burden and have a brokenness and a concern to see people saved.

I believe Moses knew what it meant to have a concern for a lost world. Moses was interceding on behalf of the people of God. In Exodus 32 God has pronounced judgment upon the people there. Then Moses began to intercede in Exodus 32:32. He said, *"Yet now, if Thou will forgive their sins—"* and he just breaks down in the middle of that sentence. By the way, sometime when you can, look at Exodus 32:32. It's the only sentence in all the Bible that is incomplete. It just cuts off right in the middle of the sentence. He's so wrapped up in emotion that he just stops and he says, *"If thou will forgive their sins,"* then he picks back up and says, *"if not, blot me, I pray Thee, out of Thy book."* In other words, he's says, "God, if you won't forgive them of their sins, just blot my name out also."

Jeremiah, the weeping prophet, knew what it meant to have a brokenness and concern for a lost world. In Lamentations 1:12, Jeremiah cried out and said, *"Is it nothing to you, all ye that pass by? Behold, and see if there be any sorrow like unto my sorrow."* Is it nothing to you? Is it nothing to you that your husband is lost? Is it nothing to you that your wife is lost? Is it nothing to you that your son or your daughter is lost? Is it nothing to you that your mom or your dad is lost? Is it nothing to you?

I heard of an evangelist years ago who was preaching along the same line that I'm preaching. After the sermon was over, a lady came up to this evangelist and said to him, "Sir, I have two older teenage sons who have never been saved. I can't understand why!" The evangelist looked back at this lady and asked, "Well, ma'am let me ask you a question. Are you saved?" She said, "Yes." He said, "Are you living for the Lord?" She said, "As much as I know how. But I cannot understand why my two sons have never been saved. Can you tell me why?" The evangelist said, "Well, let me think about it. Let me pray about it through the night. Come back tomorrow night and perhaps I'll be able to give you an answer."

The story is told that the woman came back the next night. She came to him and asked, "Sir, why have my two boys never been saved?" He said, "I'll tell you why your boys have never been saved. It's because your eyes are dry." When he said that, it was like putting a knife in her heart. She went home that night, got beside her bed and all night long she prayed and wept that her boys would be saved.

The next morning, the woman was in the kitchen. One of the boys—let his name be Jim—came through the kitchen. She said, "Jim, I'd like to talk to you." So they sat down at the table and she began to share with him about Christ and how to be saved. While she was talking to him, the other son—let his name be John—came through the kitchen and walked through the back door. She led Jim to the Lord and he was gloriously saved.

Later on in the morning, John made his way back into the house. She said to him, "John, I'd like to talk with you. I was talking to Jim a moment ago, but I'd like to talk with you." John looked back at his mother and said, "Mama, I know what you were talking to Jim about. While you were in here talking to him, I went out to the side of the garage. I got on my knees there and I cried out and asked God to save me. And God saved me. Mama, you didn't know it, but last night I walked down the hall and I saw you. I heard you praying and weeping for God to save me and Jim."

Oh, that we'd have some mothers that would baptize their bedsides with tears that their children might not go to hell. Oh, that we'd have some husbands and wives that would say, "God, I'm not going to stand before Thee unless my husband or my wife comes with me." You say, "Preacher, does it work?" Oh, it works. I could give you story after story.

Years ago, I went to be the pastor of Shiloh Baptist church in Kingston, Tennessee. There was a man in our church by the name of Bill Morton. Bill Morton was a lost man. Everybody knew Bill Morton was lost. Even he knew he was lost. He worked at the Atomic Energy Plant at Oak Ridge where they made the atomic bomb. He was a brilliant man and a very good, moral man. He was very faithful in church. He was there on Sunday morning, Sunday night, and Wednesday night. He was always there.

God began to convict and burden his wife and three daughters for Bill's salvation. It got to the point where every time I gave an invitation, the wife Mary and three daughters Connie, Theresa, and Lisa made their way to the side of the altar and huddled up just like a football team. They'd put their arms around each other and they'd get down on their knees together and they would pray and they would cry for God to save Bill.

Every service he always sat there in church. I don't know about you, but I couldn't take much of that. If I knew someone was praying that way for me, and I was sitting back there, I'd have to fish or cut bait or something. Something's going to have to give. That went on for over a year. Every service they'd come and they'd pray that way.

It was on the Sunday before Christmas and I was preaching my Christmas message. You know how it is. I'd already finished my first two points and I was getting ready to go into my third point. All of a sudden, Bill Morton stood up in the middle of the service. He started walking down the aisle. How dare him mess up my sermon that way! Oh, I knew why he was coming down. I just closed my Bible up, I met him there, and I asked, "Bill, why have you come forward?" He said, "I've come to get saved." We knelt there and he was gloriously and wonderfully saved.

About two weeks later, I was talking to Bill. I said, "Bill, you've always been a good, moral man. You've always been a good husband and a good father. Now that you're saved, what's the difference?" So simple yet so profound. Bill looked at me and he said, "Well, Preacher, I can lay my head on my pillow at night and know that if I don't wake up in the morning, I'll be with God in heaven."

I'm convinced Bill Morton got saved because he had a wife and three daughters who got hold of the horn of the altar and they would not let go until God came through. When you and I begin to get that concerned and burdened, then we're going to begin to see our loved ones come to Jesus and being saved.

3. THE COMMITMENT WE MUST MAKE TO WIN OUR UNSAVED LOVED ONES TO CHRIST.

Again, I'm convinced unless there is a definite commitment on our part to win them to Jesus, most likely they'll never be saved. Now, I'm not discounting the work of the Holy Ghost. The Spirit of God moves as He wills. He's sovereign.

What I'm saying is this: if a fisherman does not place the net in the water, he has no catch. Unless the farmer plants the seed, he has no harvest. Unless there's a definite commitment on our part to win them to Jesus, most likely they'll never be saved.

10 VERY PRACTICAL SUGGESTIONS ON HOW TO WIN YOUR UNSAVED LOVED ONES TO CHRIST.

1. **YOU NEED TO AVOID THE ATTITUDE OF A PHARISEE.** Avoid the attitude of "I have it; you don't have it." Don't come across as though you're better than they are. You'll never win them if you come across with a haughty spirit toward them.

2. **BE CAREFUL THAT WHEN YOU REJECT THE WORLD YOU DO NOT REJECT YOUR FAMILY.** The Bible does say in 2 Corinthians 6:17, *"Come out from among them and be ye separate, said the Lord, and touch not the unclean thing and I will receive you."* But you must be very careful that when you turn your back on the world, you do not turn your back on your family, too. You may be the only missionary to your family. You may be the only evangelist to your family. You're going to be able to give them a word of witness no preacher or evangelist could ever give them.

3. **AVOID HARSH, JUDGMENTAL STATEMENTS.** For example, there's a young guy who just gets saved. He walks into his home that evening after he's saved. He says, "I've got an announcement to make. I just got saved today. No

longer is anyone in our family allowed to smoke cigarettes."
Now, you are not supposed to smoke cigarettes. Don't
misread me on that. What I mean is this: if you come across
as judgmental toward them, you'll never win them to Jesus
Christ.

4. **DON'T NAG THEM.** You're not going to nag them to Jesus.
I heard about a mother who had a little toddler. She had a
hard day. Have you ever had one of those days? That little
boy had acted up all day long. You're just about to pull your
hair out and throw your hands up in the air. She had one of
those days. Out of desperation, she said, "I sure will be glad
when you grow up and get saved and won't act this way!" If
I was that little boy, I'd probably look up and say, "Well, if
that's what it means to be saved, then I don't think I want it,
thank you very much."

Do you ever find that Sunday mornings are just
tough? If there was ever a morning where Judy burnt my
toast, it was on a Sunday morning. I'm sure you're not this
way. If there was ever a morning that we had a little spat or
a little cross word, it was on a Sunday morning. Have you
ever noticed that? That's just sort of how it works. If there
was ever a morning where the kids acted up, it was on a
Sunday morning.

I have three boys who are two years apart from each
other. I want to hasten to say this so you'll understand: two
of my boys are preachers and one's a lawyer. So they did

survive. It's a wonder! Back years ago when my boys were still young, I'd always get up early in the mornings. I'd normally get up around 5:30 or 6 o' clock. I was always trying my best to be in my office by 6:30 on Sunday mornings to study and pray and get ready for the service and for the day that was ahead.

Judy was always back at home taking care of those three boys. Around Sunday School time, I'd be sitting in my office and she'd bring all three boys in two hands. She'd come running in there and throw them at me. She said, "They've about killed me this morning. Whoop-'em-all!" She didn't say, "whip them." She said, "Whoop-'em-all!" You know what I mean? You know I was in a great spirit to preach after that. Well, don't nag. You're not going to nag them to Jesus.

5. **EXPECT YOUR FAITH TO BE TESTED.** Those in your family who are unsaved will test you to see if what you have is real or not. So expect your faith to be tested.

6. **BE HONEST ABOUT YOUR MISTAKES.** You're not perfect yet. As long as you're in this life, you are still subject to sin. You're going to blow it sometime. You're not going to be perfect until you're with Jesus one day in heaven. So when you blow it, be honest about it. Just look at your family and say, "Look, I blew it. I shouldn't have said what I said. I shouldn't have acted that way. I shouldn't have done what I did. I'm sorry and I want you to forgive me." Be honest.

7. **LOVE YOUR FAMILY UNCONDITIONALLY.** This is something that is so important. This is something that God had to teach me. My father deserted my mother and I when I was just a youngster. My father left us and moved in with a bar maid with seven kids. I was raised most of my life by my grandparents because my mother wasn't able to put enough food on the table for both of us at that time. So, as a result of my father deserting us, I became very bitter and very angry at him. From the time he left us until I was a senior in high school, I never spoke to my father. If I saw him on the street, I turned my head and looked the other way. If I saw him coming down the road, if I could get out of the way quick enough, I would quickly go another direction. Year after year, I was very bitter toward him.

As a senior in high school, God called me to preach. When God called me to preach, He said to me, "I'll never use you as My preacher until you get things right with your father." So, I had to search out my father. When I found him, I said, "Dad, I want to ask you to forgive me. My attitude toward you has been just as bad, if not worse, than your actions toward us. Dad, I love you and I want you to forgive me. More than anything, I want to see you saved." Now, I'd love to say he got saved right then, but he didn't.

I went through college and my dad would come hear me preach. He would get under deep conviction, but he would not respond. Then I moved and went on to seminary out in Fort Worth, Texas. While I was there I'd call back and say, "Dad, just thinking about you. Want you to know I love you. Sure would love to see you get saved." God moved us back to East Tennessee where I pastored there after getting out of seminary. I'd have my dad come and hear me preach. He'd get under conviction. He'd hold onto the back of the pew but still he wouldn't respond.

That went on year after year after year. Seven years before my dad died, he was gloriously and wondrously saved. God set him free. God delivered him. He was an alcoholic. He was on drugs. He was married four more times after he deserted my mother and me. But God set him free and made him a new man.

Three months before he died, he was a member of my home church in Rutledge, Tennessee. When I preached a revival there, my dad packed full three or four pews every night with his old cronies he used to run with. They were the same men and women that he used to get drunk with, use drugs with, gamble with—God only knows what else. They were all there. He'd tell them, "If you go hear my son preach, I'll feed everybody after church." What that meant is they'd go over to the restaurant and he'd pay for it all. Night after night, he'd bring those folks in, and night after night, more of them got saved.

The one thing God had to show me was this: although I may not have agreed with his actions, I had to love him unconditionally. If you're going to win your loved ones to Jesus—you may not agree with what they're involved in and you may not like what they're doing—you need to let them know you love them unconditionally.

8. **DO THOUGHTFUL, NICE THINGS FOR THEM.** Kids, clean up that room that could win the City Dump Look-Alike Contest. Clean up that room without being told you need to do it. They're going to know something's up. Now men, when you come in, bring your wife a box of chocolates or roses. They're going to know something's going on.

9. **BRING THEM TO CHURCH SO THEY CAN HEAR THE GOSPEL.** It's that simple.

10. **DEPEND ON THE HOLY SPIRIT AND DON'T GIVE UP.** Don't give up, don't give up. If you're going to win your unsaved loved ones to Christ, you must determine, "No matter what the cost, no matter what the price, I'm going to win them to Jesus."

Years ago there was a family up in the north eastern part of Kentucky in the Appalachians. The wife and mother of this family was a Christian; she loved God. They had several children. Her husband was a very wicked, mean, lost man. He was the kind of guy that when a preacher came over to visit and share Christ with him, he'd cuss him out. He didn't curse him out. There's a difference. He *cussed* him out. You heard that saying, "Give someone a good cussing." Well, he gave him a bad cussing. He'd run every preacher off that way. Then he'd look at his wife and he'd tell her, "If you ever sic' a preacher on me again, I'll beat you up. Don't you ever do that again!" That's the kind of man he was.

They were having a revival there in the little church where they lived. It was a cold winter night. It was kind of icy outside. The wife went to her husband and said, "It's cold outside tonight. It's icy and sleeting. Would you mind taking me and the kids to church tonight in the old truck so we won't have to walk?" He looked back at her and said, "Listen, if you're going to church tonight, you're going to get there the best that you can. I'm not going to take you."

Well, she walked to church that night. As she made her way back, there was ice all over the road. There was a car approaching her. She moved to get out of the way of the car but she slipped on the ice and fell in the road. The oncoming car struck her and killed her instantly. The police called for her husband to come. When he got there, several cars had pulled up and the headlights lit up the scene.

He came over and he knelt down beside her body. Sticking out of her coat pocket was her Bible. He reached and pulled out the Bible. He began to thumb through the pages as the lights were shining on him. On almost every page of her Bible she had written these words: "God, if you have to take me or one of the kids to heaven, don't let Thuram go to hell."
Finally, he came over to 1 Thessalonians 5 where it says, "Pray without ceasing." Again, she had written the words, "God, if you

have to take me or one of the kids to heaven, don't let Thuram go to hell." As he was reading on that page, she had put that very day's date beneath that. Underneath, she wrote in small letters, "this may well be the day." That so gripped his heart that he came to Christ and was saved.

When you and I get to the point where we are willing to say, "God, if you have to take me to heaven, don't let my son, don't let my daughter, don't let my mama, don't let my daddy, don't let my brother, don't let my sister go to hell!" When we get to that point, then we are going to see our unsaved loved ones come to Jesus and be saved.

CHAPTER 4

BRINGING THE DEAD TO LIFE

I heard about an 85-year-old widow who called her daughter and said, "I've got a date tonight." Her daughter said, "You've got a date tonight? What do you mean you've got a date tonight?" Her mother replied, "Yes, I've got a date tonight. A man down at the Senior Citizens Center asked me out on a date tonight, so I'm going on a date."

That evening around 10 o' clock, the daughter was getting anxious about her mother. She called her mom, but no answer. The daughter called back about 11:00 and still no answer. Then she called back just shortly after midnight. Finally, her mother answered. The daughter asked, "Well, Mom. How'd the date go?"

"I had to slap that old geezer 3 times," said her mom. The daughter said, "Mom, do you mean to tell me he tried to get fresh with you?"

"No," replied her mom. "I thought he was dead!"

Well, I don't want to have to slap you to get you to come to life. But I do pray that God will indeed bring you real life. God has given us a miracle ministry, a resurrection ministry, one of bringing the dead back to life.

Open your Bible to the book of Ezekiel 37:1-10, a great passage of Scripture. I hope you are familiar with the book of

Ezekiel. Can you imagine getting to heaven one day and old Zeke coming up to you and saying, "How'd you like my book?" Don't you want to be able to say, "I liked your book"? Indeed, it is a great book.

> *"The hand of the Lord was upon me, and carried me out in the spirit of the Lord, and set me down in the midst of the valley which was full of bones, and caused me to pass by them round about: and, behold, there were very many in the open valley; and, lo, they were very dry. And He said unto me, Son of man, can these bones live? And I answered, O Lord God, Thou knowest. Again He said unto me, Prophesy upon these bones, and say unto them, O ye bones, hear the word of the Lord. Thus saith the Lord God unto these bones; Behold, I will cause breath to enter into you, and ye shall live: And I will lay sinews upon you, and will bring up flesh upon you, and cover you with skin, and put breath in you, and ye shall live; and ye shall know that I am the Lord. So I prophesied as I was commanded: and as I prophesied, there was a noise, and behold a shaking, and the bones came together, bone to his bone. And when I beheld, lo, the sinews and the flesh came up upon them, and the skin covered them above: but there was no breath in them* [that is, there was no life

in them]. *Then said He unto me, Prophesy unto the wind, prophesy, son of man, and say to the wind, Thus saith the Lord God; come from the four winds, O breath, and breathe upon these slain, that they may live. So I prophesied as He commanded me, and the breath came unto them, and they lived, and stood up upon their feet, an exceeding great army. "*

In 593 B.C. there was a prophet that was led of God to prophecy. The Bible says here in verse 1, *"The hand of the Lord was upon me. "* That is Ezekiel. In 597 B.C. Ezekiel, along with King Jehoiakim and his court, was carried into captivity by Babylon. There in Babylon, Ezekiel lived by the river Tabar. The Bible says, *"There the hand of the Lord came upon Ezekiel, "* and so Ezekiel began to prophecy. First, he prophesied in chapters 1-24 about the sins of Israel and Jerusalem and how Jerusalem would fall. Secondly, he prophesied in chapters 25-33 about the sins of the nations—specifically the sins of Tyre and Sidom and Egypt and Jerusalem. Thirdly, in chapters 34-39, he prophesied of the restoration of Israel.

Politically, we have seen that take place before our very eyes. On May 14, 1948, Israel made its way back into the land. This was a promise that God made to the Israelites in chapter 36; they would be gathered from all the nations of the world and God would bring them back together in that land which He had given to them. This was also part of the promise He made in the Abrahamic covenant.

However, in chapter 37 the Bible tells us that God took Ezekiel up on a hill and Ezekiel looked out over a valley full of dead, dry, bleached out bones. There in that valley he saw a picture of a defeated nation. He saw where Nebuchadnezzar of Babylon had defeated the armies of Israel. Not only do I want you to see the nation of Israel as a valley of dry bones, but also I want us to look at modern day America and the modern day church, a valley of dry bones. There are 4 main things I want you to see from this passage in regards to bringing the dead back to life.

1. SEEING THE REAL PROBLEM.

How are we going to have a miracle resurrection ministry? I am convinced that one reason we share so little is because we care so little. Our effectiveness and our power is going to be in direct proportion to the concern and the burden which we have. This was a broken-hearted Ezekiel. You can almost hear his burden and his brokenness as he cries out there in verse 2: *"And caused me to pass by them round about: and, behold,* [notice] *there were very many in the open valley; and, lo, they were very dry."*

I want you to go with me to a twenty-first century valley of dry bones. I believe as we look at modern day America, you see a valley of dead, dry bones. We live in a nation where anything and everything goes. We live in a nation where immorality is running rampant. We live in a nation where our children are being taught in school that premarital sex is alright, where they have taken the Bible out of the school and replaced it with condoms. We live in a nation that says that homosexuality is an accepted, inherited lifestyle. The Word of God says that homosexuality is a chosen, sinful lifestyle. It's an abomination and the judgement of God is upon it. We live in a nation where over 50% of the marriages in America end up in a divorce. It's almost as easy to get a divorce as picking up today's newspaper. We live in a nation where the victim is arrested for protecting himself and the criminal is set free. We live in a nation where Hollywood flushes its toilets into our living rooms. Night after night they're spewing their smut with sex and cursing and violence into our homes. If that offends you, then just get right with God about it. As people of God, we need to be willing to stand up and say, "For me and my house, we're not going to watch that stuff." I don't know about your television set, but my television set has an on and off switch.

We live in a nation where if you break an eagle's egg, they will fine you $5,000 because they say there's a little eaglet in there. Yet we pay doctors in their abortion clinics to murder unborn babies. We live in a nation which says it's alright to drink your alcohol, to gamble, to have your affairs. Then we say, "God bless America." I believe it's time to say, "America, bless God!" This was a broken-hearted Ezekiel. You and I need to be broken-hearted over the conditions of America today.

The only hope for America is God. At the same time, the greatest threat to America is God. Unless America repents and comes back to Him, we face the certain judgement of God. I want you to walk with me a little further into this battle. I want you to look through the eyes of Ezekiel as he looks upon that valley of dry bones. There he sees the dead. I want you to look around and I want you to see the dead. I hear some people say, "We live in a sick world." This is not a sick world; this is a dead world. We don't just need spiritual vitamins, we need resurrection! Those without Christ are dead in sin. Ephesians 2:1 says, *"And you hath he quickened* [that is, made alive] *who were dead in trespasses and sins."* Look at the dead around you, the walking, talking, living dead. Bodies walking, mouths talking, eyes seeing, ears hearing, but they're dead! They don't have the life of Christ. You and I need to understand they're only going to come to life in response to the burden and concern which we have for them.

It's been a long time since I've seen people really broken over lost people. It used to be people would weep over lost souls being saved. A lot of us were raised in the mountains where we'd have the old mourner's bench. I want to tell you something, friend: we need to learn how to mourn over lost souls again.

When I was pastor at Roebuck Park Baptist Church in Birmingham, I had a lady who came into my office one day by the name of Donna Light. Donna came in and she sat across from my desk. She said to me, "Pastor, I have a daughter who lives up

72

in Detroit. My daughter is lost and I want you to pray that she'll be saved." Being the pastor that I thought I needed to be, I said, "OK, I'll pray for her." I had a sweet little pastor's prayer and I said, "Lord, save Donna's daughter, amen." She looked back at me and said, "Pastor, I told you my daughter is lost and I want you to PRAY for her!" I thought, "Okay." I'll put a little more intensity into it. I said, "Oh, God! Donna's daughter is lost and she needs to get saved!" All of a sudden I heard Donna Light slip off the couch. She began to cry out and say, "Oh, God! My girl's lost and she's going to hell. God, don't let her go to hell!" God began to speak to my heart. That's what it means when we really get burdened over lost souls.

Let me tell you the good news. That Sunday morning, I gave the invitation. I looked toward the back of the church. Here came Donna Light with a young lady on her arm. She walked down that aisle with a big smile on her face. She said, "Preacher, this is my daughter from Detroit. Tell her how to get saved." When we begin to pray that way, we begin to get that kind of burden and we begin to see lost people come to know Christ. When we begin to pray that way, we begin to see the Spirit of God fall on our services. We begin to see people come under conviction once again. How long has it been since you've seen people really get under conviction at a church service? They couldn't wait, they had to come!

A few years ago I was preaching at an outdoor crusade in a tent in Dayton, Ohio. Toward the middle of the week, I preached a pretty tough message. When I gave the invitation, I looked over the congregation and down came a young black boy, 16 or 17 years old. He was all slumped over. He had a hood on his head and his hands were in his pockets—and in the middle of July! I thought, "He's going to shoot me!" He came down and literally just fell on the altar. I thought, "He's been slain in the Spirit and I don't even believe it!" I saw one of the workers in the church walk over and kneel there with him. Before long, I saw the worker lead him to Christ. After the invitation was over, I walked over and asked him, "What in the world took place? Why'd you just fall down that way?" He said, "Preacher, I was so struck with conviction that I was such a sinner and God loved me so much that He would save me. I couldn't stand up." That next night that young man was there, bright-eyed, a smile on his face. He ran up to me. He said, "Preacher, I've got Momma and Daddy back there with me tonight. I'm going to get baptized Sunday night." He asked, "Will you come and see me get baptized?" When you and I begin to get a burden for lost folks, we begin to see them come to Jesus. We need to look at the dead and realize they're only going to be raised, they're only going to be saved in regard to the burden that we have over them.

I want you to walk a little further with me in this valley. Ezekiel said, "I began to preach what God told me to preach." You know what took place? Remember the old song? The toe bone connected to the foot bone and the foot bone connected to the ankle bone and the ankle bone connected to the leg bone. All those bones began to come together. There was a shaking. There was a rattling in that valley and the sinews came together and the flesh came together. Now Ezekiel is not just looking at bones but he is looking now at glassy-eyed corpses. This can be deceptive. There's no doubt that when you see a bone, there's death. But when you look at a corpse, it can be deceptive. This was a corpse without breath, without life. I don't want to read too much into this but I believe God is giving us a picture of the modern day church. I believe as God looks at the modern day church, He's looking at a corpse, a body but with no breath and no life. Do you remember in Revelation Jesus was writing to the church of Sardis? He said to the church of Sardis, "Boys, you've got a pretty good reputation. You've got a pretty good name. Things are going okay over there. But, I've checked your vital signs and you're dead."

Oh, how we need the breath of the Holy Spirit to fall upon us. So often we think that as long as we've got everything else going, everything's ok. For far too long we, as Southern Baptists, think all we need is just another program, just another cog in the wheel. But we don't need just another program. We need life from the Holy Spirit. That's the need in our day. Ezekiel was broken-hearted. He looked upon bodies with no breath. Does it not burden you—does it not break your heart— to realize a church can go through all of its activities and still not have the life of God upon it? You can have liturgy without life, programs without power. You can be perfectly organized and be dead. The most organized place, easily, is the grave yard and it's dead. Oh, how we need the life of God upon us.

I don't know about you but I despise high church formalism. You may think I'm not formal enough. If you realized how much effort I had to put forth to be as constrained as I am, you'd appreciate what little bit does seep out. You go into many churches today, you can't even sneeze unless the bulletin has three stars out beside it and says, "sneeze here." Everything has to go according to our pre-printed, pre-planned, often-times lifeless program.

I can almost imagine a funeral taking place. There's an old boy in the casket. All of a sudden he comes to life. He kicks the lid off of the casket. He sits up in the casket and he says, "Wait a minute! I'm alive! I'm alive!" If it were in the average Baptist church, the ushers would march forward, push him back in the casket, fasten the lid back down and say, "That's not in the program today." I'm not talking about anything out in left field here. I know the Bible says, "Where the Spirit of the Lord is, there is liberty!"

You say, "Are you a Baptist?" I'm a Baptist, but I'm not a dead one. I was raised in a mountain Southern Baptist church. It comes out of my background. We'd have church. We'd clap. We'd even raise our hands. We'd shout. We'd shout like Baptists shout. We did that before it ever became popular. Oh, how we need to just get back to our roots. A lot of people have the idea today that if you get a little excited or if you get a little gumption, you're getting away from where the convention would have you to be. I want to remind you Southern Baptists were born from a people who had a heart on fire for God, who had a heart burdened for souls because they had a fervency for God. How long has it been since something's taken place in your church that could not be explained in human terms? How long has it been since Holy God has touched down in this place and the only way you could explain it was, "God did it"? That's what we're looking for. When we leave church we want to talk about how God showed up. The only way that's going to happen is if we begin to look and see the real problem. There's a dead, dry valley of bones and they're only going to be raised in response to the burden which you and I have.

2. SEEING THE SERIOUSNESS OF THE REAL PRICE.

Ezekiel said, *"The hand of the Lord was upon me."* Can you say, "The hand of the Lord is upon me?" I don't know about you, but I don't want any place in ministry unless I can say, "The hand of the Lord is upon me." If the hand of the Lord is not on me, I want out of it. Notice a couple of things about the seriousness of the real price.

- **THE PERSON GOD IS GOING TO USE IN HIS MINISTRY.** The only way God is going to use you in His ministry is you've got to get honest. Let me tell you the reason a lot of people and a lot of churches don't have a resurrection ministry. They just keep sweeping the dirt and the junk under the rug. The Bible says the Spirit of

77

the Lord was upon me—the Holy Spirit. The only way we're going to see the resurrection ministry is if we are holy people. Maybe you have allowed junk to build up in your own life through the days. Maybe, as a church, you've allowed junk to build up. Many people just come forward and they say, "God bless me anyhow." God's not going to bless you anyhow. The only way God's going to bless, and the only way we're going to see revival sweep through this church, is we've got to be holy. We've got to come clean with God.

- **THE PLACE GOD IS GOING TO USE YOU.** This amazed me as I read this passage again. Did you notice where God placed Ezekiel? He just dropped him right down there in the middle of that valley of dry bones. He's rubbing shoulders with the dead. Are you willing to get out there and rub shoulders with those living in trespasses and sin? Our problem is that we want to do all of our evangelizing in the church building. We want to do it from the pulpit or from the choir loft or from the classroom. The average Baptist church has what I call Mae West evangelism. For those of us who are old enough to remember, she used to say, "Why don't you come up and see me sometime?" That's what the church is saying: "Come hear our preacher. Come hear our choir. Come hear our teachers." They've not come and they're not going to come. Jesus said, "As My Father has sent Me, even so, send I you." We need to have spirit of C.D. Studd. He said, "Many want to build their house within the shadow of the chapel steeple but I want to build a rescue house on the banks of hell." That's the way Jesus was. He got out there and rubbed shoulders with the dead, the prostitutes, the drunks, the outcasts. And He says, "As the Father has sent me, so send I you."

I read an article some time back from one of our state papers and it troubled me. It told about a preacher that felt led of God to have a ministry at a race track where they would race these drag cars. He would go there and preach to those race car drivers. There was a man who wrote back in and said that he could not believe that this preacher would lower the Gospel so low that he would go out there to where those men would race those old cars and preach the Gospel. When I read that I thought, "Has that man ever read the New Testament? Did he ever read about Jesus?" The first person He led to Himself was a woman who'd been married five times and the man she was sleeping with right then wasn't even her husband. The last person He won before He went to glory was the thief on the cross. It was pretty much that way all in between. I want to say to that preacher, "Go to those men who drive those race cars and take the Gospel to them." Let him go! Ninety-five percent of the lost world out there will never walk into a church by themselves. If they are ever going to be won, we've got to go out there where they are.

3. SEEING THE SUBMISSIVENESS TO THE REAL PLAN.

What's involved in God's plan for having a resurrection ministry? Two things:

- **PREACHING.** Ezekiel said, "I prophesied, I preached as I was told to preach. I preached to them and they began to come together." As a 17-year-old boy, God called me to preach. I'll be honest with you, when God called me to preach I said, "God, it's that guy next to me, not me." I was scared to death. I thought preachers were weird. I've come to the conviction it's only through the foolishness of preaching that the lost are going to be saved. It doesn't bother me one bit just to stand up and preach the Word of God. It's only through the preaching of the Word of God that we are going to see the lost saved and the church come alive. I'm praying that God is going to call a host of young men out of the church across America, to see them trained and sent forth to preach the Gospel. Maybe you're one of them and God's already speaking to your heart. There are some adult men where God called you years ago but you turned back. You need to come back and do what God told you to do. I'm just praying that God's going to call men out to preach the Word of God.

This message is primarily to preachers but there's a message here for every Christian, also. You see, we all have the message. Do you know your message? It's Jesus. I love to read biographies. I was reading some time back a biography about John Wesley, the founder of the Methodist church. There was a day when the Methodist church was on fire for souls. In that biography it gave a little diary in a day in Wesley's life. Wesley said, "I rode into town and I preached Jesus and they threw me out. I rode into town and I went to the church and I preached Jesus and they ran me off." You and I may not be able to ride into town on a horse, but as we go to work, as we go to school, as we go out in our community activities, give them Jesus. Give them Jesus! Wherever you go, give them Jesus.

I went out to eat with a pastor one time. We came across a young man named Joshua. We gave him Jesus. Another time, I met a young lady name Julie working at a motel. She said she had a sickness. I said, "I know Someone who can take care of that sickness." She asked, "Who's that?" I said, "The Great Physician, Jesus. He can give you a new heart." She said, "Oh, I need a new heart." People are out there. They're all around. Give them Jesus.

- **PRAYER.** Notice that Ezekiel said in verse 7, *"So I prophesied as I was commanded: and I prophesied, there* *was a noise, and behold a shaking, and the bones came together, bone to his bone."* Then in verse 9 he says, *"Thus saith the Lord God; Come from the four winds, O breath, and breathe upon these slain, that they may live."* There's never been a movement of God that was not birthed through prayer. The Bible says, in the early church of Acts 4:31:

> *"And when they had prayed, the place was shaken where they were assembled together; and they were all filled with the Holy Ghost and they spake the Word of God with boldness."*

The God that shook that valley in Ezekiel's day, the God that shook that early church, is still in the shaking business. Wouldn't you like to see your church shaken by the prayers of God's people? If it's going to take place, it's going have to take place at the altar as God's people get on their face before Him.

I don't know what you do after Sunday School. If you sing in the choir, you go to the choir. If you are an usher, you usher. If you don't have anything else to do between Sunday School and worship, find a place to pray. Many churches have prayer rooms now, so for those 5 or so minutes, just meet there and pray. Just get on your face there and pray for the service. You don't have to be a deacon, a teacher, or whatever. Just pray. Pray for the anointing upon your church and that God would shake the place. Pray for your pastor and his preaching, that God would use him in a mighty way. Believe me, you'll see a difference in your pastor. When you pray for your pastor like that, he can just about take on hell with a water pistol! You'll see God do something!

4. SEEING THE SUCCESS OF THE REAL POWER.

Let's look at verse 10. The Bible says, *"So I prophesied as He commanded me, and the breath came into them, and they lived, and stood upon their feet, an exceeding great army."* What took place? One word: life. No longer bones, no longer glassy-eyed corpses but now life—an exceeding great army. When we open up our eyes and we get a burden, and we come clean with God and we begin to pray, we're going to see life. We're going to see the lost being saved. We're going to see revival sweep through the church, an exceeding, mighty army.

There's something else I see here. Not only do I see an exceeding great army here upon the earth, but I see also a reunion there in heaven one day around the throne of God. Imagine when you show up in heaven, someone walks over to you and they say, "I've been waiting on you. I want to thank you for telling me about Jesus, because if it were not for you, I wouldn't be here. Oh, I know that I was unkind to you at first, but you just loved me through it all. Finally, I gave my heart to Jesus. I want to thank you for telling me about Jesus." Then we take our crowns and we cast them at the feet of Jesus, the crucified One, now reigning as King of Kings and Lord of Lords.

We will join our voices with a great host of heaven saying, "Worthy is the Lamb that was slain to receive power, riches, wisdom, strength, honor, glory, and blessing forever and ever. Amen. Hallelujah. Hallelujah!"

I say today, "Son of man, can these bones live again?" May we hear God say, "And they stood an exceeding mighty army." May God grant it!

CHAPTER 5

LOOKING INTO HEAVEN

A wife sat up straight in her bed in the middle of the night. She was crying and screaming. Finally, her husband woke up. He tried to comfort her. He asked her, "Why are you so upset?" She said, "I had a dream. I dreamed that I went to heaven. In heaven, they were having a husband auction. Some husbands were auctioned off for $1,000, other husbands were auctioned for $2,000." Curiosity got the best of her husband and he asked, "Well, what were husbands like me going for?" She began to cry even more. Finally, when she regained her composure, she said, "husbands like you were bundled together, 3 bundles for $1."

Well, I don't believe we'd see anything like that in heaven. I want to preach on the subject of "Looking into Heaven." Open your Bible to Revelation 21:1-8.

> *"And I saw a new heaven and a new earth: for the first heaven and the first earth were passed away; and there was no more sea. And I John saw the Holy city, new Jerusalem, coming down from God out of heaven, prepared as a bride adorned for her husband. And I heard a great voice out of heaven saying, Behold, the tabernacle of God is with men, and He will dwell with them, and they shall be His people, and God*

Himself shall be with them, and be their God. And God shall wipe away all tears from their eyes; and there shall be no more death, neither sorrow, nor crying, neither shall there be any more pain: for the former things are passed away. And He that sat upon the throne said, Behold, I make all things new. And He said unto me, Write: for these words are true and faithful. And He said unto me, It is done. I am Alpha and Omega, the beginning and the end. I will give unto him that is athirst of the fountain of the water of life freely. He that overcometh shall inherit all things; and I will be his God, and he shall be My son. But the fearful, and unbelieving, and the abominable, and murderers, and whore-mongers, and sorcerers, and idolaters, and all liars, shall have their part in the lake which burneth with fire and brimstone: which is the second death."

William Booth, who was the founder of the Salvation Army, had a person come to him on one occasion. The person said, "Mr. Booth, I'm convinced that the training you give to your personal soul winners is the best training there is available today." Being the humble man that he was, William Booth responded by saying, "Thank you very much for saying that. Although the training I give to our personal soul winners may be the best there is available today, it's not the best training there is for a soul winner. The best training would be for a person to spend five minutes in hell. Then he would be a soul winner."

I believe he was exactly right. If a person could just get a glimpse of hell, it would do away with the casual, don't-care attitude that so many Christians have in regards to witnessing and soul winning. Yet, I don't want us to look into hell; I want us to look into heaven. I believe if we could just get a glimpse of heaven, it will literally change our lives.

When you get an interest in a place, you want to find out everything you can about it. As an evangelist, I travel week after week to different places. When I know I'm going to a new place, I try to find out everything I can about it. I get to go to some interesting places. For example, have you ever heard of Pumpkintown, South Carolina? It's a great big place at the foot of Table Rock, North Carolina. There's only one red light, and when it's turned on, it blinks. I preached a camp meeting there a few years back. To be honest with you, it didn't take long to learn everything there was to know about Pumpkintown, South Carolina.

Have you ever heard of Frog Jump, Tennessee? Over in west Tennessee, north of Memphis, I preached a revival in Curve, Tennessee. On the way to Curve, I had to drive through Frog Jump every night. Have you ever heard of Bug Tussle, Texas? It's right outside Dail, Texas, which is right outside Honey Grove, Texas. I preached a revival outside Bug Tussle. Now, in Bug Tussle, there is one building. One building! It is the grocery store, the post office, the restaurant—everything that is in that town is in that one building. In that building, they have banners that say, "The Bug Tussle Tusslers." There are banners for a ball team they don't even have!

There's another place I have great interest in. The reason I have such great interest in that place is because there are some people there who are very dear to me. I have a wife who is there. I have a mother and a father and a little 3-year-old sister who are there. I have dear friends who are there. It is that City of God, that City of David, that new Jerusalem, that place where Jesus is with the Father. Maybe you have a mother, father, brother, sister, son, or daughter who is in heaven. That should give you reason to want to find out everything you can about that glorious place!

I want us to look into heaven. I want us to see what is taking place in heaven right now. Not what has taken place in heaven, or what is going to take place in heaven, but what is taking place in heaven right now.

1. LOOK AND SEE WHAT THE SUPERNATURAL BEINGS ARE DOING IN HEAVEN.

God has His holy angels. I heard two men talking the other day. One man said to the other man, "I believe my wife is an angel." The other man replied, "Now, wait a minute. I know your wife is a very nice lady and a godly lady. But don't you believe you're stretching it a bit to say your wife is an angel?" The first man said, "Well, she has to be an angel because she's always up there harping about something."

What are the angels doing in heaven, though?

- **They're shouting praises to His precious name.** Look back at Revelation 5:11-12:

> *"And I beheld, and I heard the voice of many angels round about the throne and the beasts and the elders: and the number of them was ten thousand times ten thousand, and thousands of thousands; saying with a loud voice, Worthy is the Lamb that was slain to receive power, and riches, and wisdom, and strength, and honour, and glory, and blessing."*

The name of Jesus is worthy to be praised. Isn't it strange we can get excited about everything else in the world? We'll go out in the fall of the year to a big ol' pasture field on a Saturday afternoon and we'll watch 22 men chase a bag of air up and down the field. They'll almost kill each other. Now, I'm not making fun of sports. I like sports. I can whoop and holler with the best of them. But isn't it strange that we can get so excited on a Saturday afternoon and act like Comanche Indians, and then we'll come to church on Sunday morning and sit there like a bunch of dead wooden Indians? The name of Jesus is worthy to be praised!

I made up my mind a long time ago that I'll never let the angels out-praise me. You know why? Angels don't know what it means to be redeemed by the blood of the Lamb. Angels don't know what it means to be saved by the grace of God. Angels don't know what it is to experience God's great salvation. If anyone ought to be praising God, it ought to be the people of God!

- **The angels are serving the King for the kingdom.** I believe if we were to look into heaven, we would see God look over to one of His angels and say, "Angel, there's one of my children in trouble. Go, watch over and protect them!" You ask, "Do you really believe that?" Oh, not only do I believe it, I can prove it.

  ○ *"The angel of the Lord encampeth round about them that fear him, and delivereth them."* – Psalm 34:7

  ○ *"For He shall give His angels charge over thee, to keep thee in all thy ways."* – Psalm 91:11

I can give you story after story. For example, Dr. Sam Cathy is a Southern Baptist evangelist. He is now 81 years old. His health is beginning to fail. He's been a dear, dear friend to me throughout the years. Brother Sam is one of those evangelists who will skin you alive, then throw in salt. That's just the type of preaching that he does. I'd always kid with him. I'd say, "Sam, it takes at least six archangels just to watch over you and keep you out of trouble." That's the kind of preacher he is.

He tells about preaching a series of revival meetings in Michigan. He'd been up there for 3 weeks. At the end of the third week, he was looking forward to getting back home to see his wife and 3 daughters. He went to the airport and had his ticket. He walked up to the ticket agent and said, "I'd like to get a boarding pass and a seat assignment." The agent looked back and said, "We're having some problems and mechanical difficulties with the plane. It's going to be a little while. Go and get yourself something to eat and come back."

Brother Sam said he went off and got himself a few hotdogs and a couple sodas. He finally made his way back and gave his ticket to the agent. Again, he said he wanted a boarding pass and a seat assignment. The ticket agent said, "What are you doing here?" Sam said, "I want on that plane." The agent replied, "You're already on that plane." He said, "Well, I'm here, ain't I?" The agent looked back and said, "Listen, I put you on that plane, and that plane has already left. You were on that plane!"

Brother Sam said later that afternoon, he heard where that same plane crashed. Every person on that plane was killed. Brother Sam is convinced that God sent an angel to take his place. Now, that's what he believes. You can believe what you want to believe, and I can believe what I want to believe. But I do know this much: from time to time, God will send angels out to watch over and protect the people of God.

2. **LOOK AND SEE WHAT THE SAVIOR IS DOING IN HEAVEN.**

- **Jesus is praying petitions for the saints.** I believe if we could look into heaven, we'd see Jesus seated at the right hand of the Father. What's He doing? He's praying for me. He's praying for you.

  ○ *"Wherefore He is able also to save them to the uttermost that come unto God by Him, seeing He ever liveth to make intercession for them."* – Hebrews 7:25

  ○ *"My little children, these things write I unto you, that you sin not. And if any man sin, we have an advocate with the Father, Jesus Christ the righteous."* – I John 2:1

Jesus is my advocate. Jesus is my attorney. Jesus is my lawyer. He's never lost a case, and He'll never lose a case. Even after we're saved, we still sin. We're not going to be perfect until we go be with Jesus in heaven one day. As long as we're in this life, we're still subject to sin. By the way, that's one of the best ways to know if you're saved or not. You can't get by with your sin. When you sin as a Christian, there's going to be an alarm going off in your heart and in your spirit to let you know where you're going, how you're living, or the way you're talking is wrong. Even as a Christian, when we sin or do wrong, it's as if Jesus looks to the Father and says, "Father, remember! They're part of the family." When Don Whitt sins—and I do—it's as if Jesus looks to the Father and says, "Father, remember! He's part of the family." The

Bible goes on to say in Romans 8:34, *"Who is He that condemneth? It is Christ that died, yea rather, that is risen again, Who is even at the right hand of God, Who also maketh intercession for us."* When we sin as a Christian, it's almost as if we feel the condemnation of the devil coming down on us. It's as if the devil rushes in on the presence of God and says, "Look there at your child! Look there at the one calling themselves, 'Christian.' I demand the death penalty for them!" Oh, but God the Father looks over to the Son and remembers that day when Jesus went to Calvary and paid the sin debt with His own precious blood. When God looks at us, He sees us through the blood and the righteousness of Jesus Christ. I am thankful that I have a Friend in heaven who is praying for me. His name is Jesus.

- **Jesus is preparing a place for the saints.** John 14:2 says, *"In My Father's house are many mansions: if it were not so, I would have told you. I go to prepare a place for you."* Heaven is a real place. Heaven is just as real as the church where we gather. Heaven is not just some ghostly myth out there in Yonder Land. Heaven is a real place.

    "Well, don't you believe Jesus could just speak a word and there would be a mansion," you ask? Oh yes. In fact, He wouldn't even have to speak a word. All He'd have to do is just think about it and it would be done.

"What do you think that mansion is going to look like?"

It's going to look a lot like a mansion.

"Do you really believe there's going to be streets of gold?"

Oh, yes.

"Do you believe there's going to be walls of jasper?"

Oh, yes.

"Do you believe there's going to be gates of pearl?"

Oh, yes.

"Do you believe there's going to be a sea of crystals?"

Oh, yes.

"Oh, what an imagination you have!"

Hey, if it's not going to be like that, then it's going to be better!

- **Jesus is personally present with the saints.** The Bible teaches that when a Christian dies, they go immediately into the presence of God. I made that statement some time back and after the service, there was a person who came up to me and said, "Don't ever make that statement again." I asked, "What statement?" He said, "That statement that when a person dies, they go immediately into the presence of God." Now this is what he said to me: "The Bible teaches that when a Christian dies, their body goes back to the grave and their soul stays in that grave and sleeps until Jesus comes back again." The only thing wrong with that is this: that's wrong. The Bible teaches that when a Christian dies, they go immediately into the presence of God. Let me give you 4 passages that bears that out so clearly for you.

- **Matthew 22:32.** The Sadducees have come to Jesus and they're asking Him questions trying to trick Him. Do you remember who the Sadducees were? They were the liberals of that day. They did not believe in the resurrection, miracles, or angels. They did not believe in the supernatural things of God. You know why they were called Sadducees? They were sad, you see. All liberals are sad. If you don't believe in the supernatural things of God, how in the world are you going to have the joy of the Lord? So, they were asking Jesus these trick questions. They asked, "If a woman's been married many times, whose wife is she going to be in heaven?" I like His answer. In essence, He said, "Not going to be any marriages in heaven. And to be honest with you, there aren't too many marriages that are very heavenly down here." But then Jesus said in verse 32, *"I am the God of Abraham, and the God of Isaac, and the God of Jacob. God is not the God of the dead, but of the living."* Abraham is still alive. Isaac is still alive. Jacob is still alive. Once you trust Jesus and God saves you, you never die! One day this body will die. This ol' tabernacle where we live will die. But the real you will never die!

- **Matthew 17.** On the mount of transfiguration, the disciples saw Jesus, and with Jesus were Moses and

Elijah. They passed off the scene hundreds of years before that. Yet, the disciples looked and said, "There's Jesus and Moses and Elijah."

- **Luke 23:43**. When He was hanging upon the cross, Jesus looked over to that dying thief and said unto him, *"Verily I say unto thee, today shalt thou be with me in paradise."* Today! You say, "Now preacher, don't you know that in a very technical sense there is a difference between heaven and paradise?" I've been studying the Bible seriously since I was 17 years old. You know what conclusion I've come up with? Wherever Jesus is, that's heaven enough for me.

- **2 Corinthians 5:8**. Paul said, *"We are confident, I say, and willing rather to be absent from the body, and to be present with the Lord."* This last year some of us followed the casket of a loved one out to the graveyard. We saw them plant that casket into the ground. I've got a good word for you and for me. That loved one, if they were saved, aren't in that casket. They're not in that grave. Absent from the body is to be present with the Lord. That gives us comfort at the time of the death of a loved one.

3. **LOOK AND SEE WHAT THE SAINTS ARE DOING IN HEAVEN.**

Would you like to know what Christians are doing in heaven right now? Let me give you a word of warning: if you have any bit of Bapti-costal in you whatsoever, you better fasten your seat belt because you're not going to be able to sit still for very long. If this doesn't bless you, then your "Blesser" is already worn out. What are the Christians doing in heaven?

- **They are worshiping the worthiness of Christ.**
  - *"And after these things I heard a great voice of much people in heaven, saying, Alleluia; Salvation and glory, and honour, and power, unto the Lord our God."* – Revelation 19:1
  - *"And the four and twenty elders and the four beasts fell down and worshipped God that sat on the throne, saying, Amen; Alleluia."* – Revelation 19:4

Wouldn't you love to get in a service like that? People are shouting, "Amen! Hallelujah! Praise the Lord! Thank You, Jesus!" If that bothers you, you're going to have real problems in heaven. While I'm telling you something, I'll tell you something else. I really don't think there are going to be any printed bulletins in heaven. If that bothers you, you better check up and see if your oil's been changed. I really don't believe the service is going to be over 12 o' clock noon on Sundays. You say, "It's not down here either!" Oh, can you imagine what it will be like to worship God that way? I'm just simple-minded about this. If I'm going to spend an eternity worshiping and praising and adoring Jesus in heaven, I ought to practice up on it down here. You know, a lot of people are going to be as out of place in heaven as a screen door on a submarine. They're not going to know how to enjoy heaven because they've never learned how to really worship and praise God.

A while back, I preached a revival at Mount Ararat Baptist Church in Trezevant, Tennessee. Mount Ararat Baptist Church is an African-American church. Trezevant, Tennessee has about 100 people in the city and that church runs over 300 every week. All the African-American believers in the area come to that church. It's a great, wonderful church. They know how to worship! But they just about killed me. I'd get to preaching, and they'd get to singing back to me. I'd get in this rhythm with them. I even sang it back to them, and I can't sing! Finally, on the last night of the revival, I looked at them and said, "Folks, I wish I could just box you up and take you to a bunch of these dead white churches I have to preach in every week."

I preached there one night and I was in a rocking and waving way. A dear older lady sat in the front row. Glory got all over her. She just jumped up and started dancing and going 'round and 'round. I thought I was in Africa again. All of a sudden she turned loose and ran all the way around the auditorium. I just kept on preaching. When the service was over, 2 of my white brethren came up to me and said, "Preacher, didn't that bother you when that woman ran that way?" I said, "Goodness no! If I weren't so out of shape, I'd run with her!" In heaven, we're going to be worshiping the worthiness of God.

- **They are praising the provision of Christ.** Just think of some of the provisions that they're praising Christ for:

98

○ **They're praising Him for the provision of rest.** Revelation 14:13 says:

> *"And I heard a voice from heaven saying unto me, Write, Blessed are the dead which die in the Lord from henceforth: Yea, saith the Spirit, that they may rest from their labours; and their works do follow them."*

Good works do not get you into heaven. You are saved by grace through faith in Jesus Christ—plus or minus nothing. But your works are going to follow you into heaven. Sometimes there will be a person who will walk down the aisle and say, "Pastor, here's my ticket. Punch it so I can go to heaven." Then they go out and live like the devil. They live immoral lives. They drink, curse and turn their backs on God, the church of God, and the things of God. Then they have the idea that one day when they die, they're going to step over into heaven as the perfect Apostle Paul. No way! If you live like the devil here, that's a good indication you're going to the devil when you die. You and I ought to live in such a way that when we step over into heaven one day, others will say, "There's a man, there's a woman, there's a young person that was totally sold out to Jesus Christ!" This is no time for lackadaisical, lukewarm, take-it-or-leave-it Christians. This is a time to be all-out, whole-hog for Jesus!

○ **They're praising Him for the provision of service.**
Revelation 7:15 says:

> *"Therefore are they before the throne of God,*
> *and serve Him day and night in His temple: and*
> *He that sitteth on the throne shall dwell among*
> *them."*

Heaven is a place of activity, not inactivity. God's not going to put you out on some fluffy cloud somewhere and give you a harp to pluck and angel wings to flop about for all eternity. Heaven's going to be a place of activity where we can serve Him. Do you ever get involved in things down here that you really like to do? You get involved in something you're doing, then the phone will ring. With these cell phones, you can't get away from it. Or the doorbell will ring. Men, you think all week long when Saturday finally comes around you've got something you want to do on Saturday. But when Saturday finally comes around, your honey has some honeydos she wants you to do. Oh, in heaven we're going to be able to serve Him day and night, night and day. Never get tired! Never get weary! No Geritol, no halitol, no vitamin B. We're going to be able to serve Him forever and ever!

○ **They're praising Him for the provision of healing.**
Look again in Revelation 21:4: *"And God shall wipe away all tears from their eyes; and there shall be no*

more death, neither sorrow, nor crying, neither shall there be any more pain: for the former things are passed away." Last time some of us saw our loved ones, they were being dragged down to the grave with cancer. But there's no cancer in heaven. There are no heart attacks in heaven. There is no blindness in heaven. There are no cripples in heaven. In heaven, we're going to have perfect health forever and ever.

- **They are expecting the entrance of Christ.** First Corinthians 15:51-52 says:

  "Behold, I shew you a mystery; We shall not all sleep, but we shall all be changed, in a moment, in the twinkling of an eye, at the last trump: for the trumpet shall sound and the dead shall be raised incorruptible, and we shall be changed."

You say, "Now wait a minute, Preacher. Are you saying that when a Christian dies and they go to heaven, now they have a spirit body?" Yes, that's right. When they die, when they go to heaven, they have a spirit body. I don't know exactly what it looks like, but I guess it probably looks better than most of us do right now. One of these days, the Father is going to look over at His Son and say, "Jesus, go get Your church! Go get Your bride! Go get Your body!" The Bible says the Lord will descend from heaven with a shout and a voice of the archangel and the trumpet of God. All the saved of all the ages will be caught up to meet the Lord in the air! We're going to be given a new body liken to His glorious body! What a day that is going to be! I can almost imagine in heaven right now the saints are looking to Jesus saying, "Jesus, when are You going to get Your church?" And He's saying, "Just a little longer. Just a little longer."

- **They are rejoicing over the redemption through Christ.** Christians in heaven rejoice when souls get saved here on earth. You ask, "Do you really believe that?" Oh, not only do I believe it, but I can prove it. Over in Luke 15, Jesus tells us of three lost things. He tells us of the lost sheep, the lost coin, and the lost son. Notice what happened when the sheep was found in verse 7:

> *"I say unto you, that likewise joy shall be in heaven over one sinner that repenteth, more than over ninety and nine just persons, which need no repentance."*

Then notice what happened when the coin was found in verse 10: *"Likewise, I say unto you, there is joy in the presence of the angels of God over one sinner that repenteth."* Notice not that the angels are rejoicing, but there's joy in the *presence* of the angels. Who's that? That's the saved; that's the Christians. Also, notice what happened when that lost, prodigal son came back home. Notice what the Father said in verse 24-25:

> *"For this my son was dead and is alive again; he*

was lost, and is found. And they began to be
merry. Now his elder son was in the field: and as
he came and drew nigh to the house, he heard
music and dancing."

He heard music and dancing! You say, "Well he must not have been a Baptist." When souls get saved, you can dance all you want for the glory of God over souls being saved. You say, "Well, that's not very Baptistic." No, but it's the Bible.

A few years ago I was in South Africa and we were preaching out in this great, big village. My team built a church building there while I was preached at a tent crusade every night. In fact, the people who were getting saved in the tent crusade were actually becoming the new church who we were building for. I have to be honest: I am dangerous with a hammer and a saw. I could do more damage in 30 minutes than the whole crew could fix all week long. So they told me, "Preacher, just go on and do your thing. You go on and preach and we'll build the church."

Every morning I would go and preach in the public schools there in South Africa. I don't think you heard me. I went and preached in the public schools in South Africa! I gave an invitation and they got saved! God have mercy on America. One afternoon I had some of the men that came to me and said, "Preacher, would you like to go to one of the neighboring villages and preach this afternoon?" I said I'd love to. We loaded up the sound equipment and got the keyboard and loaded it up in the back of the truck and got a power generator. We drove about 30 or 35 miles over to a neighboring village. It was a great big village with probably 30,000-40,000 people. There were two main roads in the village. We set up right in that intersection.

They started playing the keyboard and you could hear that thing probably 20 miles away. People started coming from everywhere. They began to praise and sing and worship. That went on for a while. Finally, I stepped up and, through an interpreter, I preached the very simple message of how to be saved. I gave an invitation and out of that crowd came over 25 adults who were gloriously saved.

They cranked up that power generator again and they began to play the keyboard. They began to sing and praise God. They began to dance, too! You'd be proud of me. I was a good Baptist boy. I stood there and tapped my foot and patted my hand. I was happy! A big African man came over to me and asked, "Preacher not happy?" I said, "Preacher happy!" He said, "If Preacher happy, why he not dance?" I said, "Whoo, let's go! Let's get with it!"

You say, "Well, I'm just not the emotional type." Yes, you are. When something is important to you, you get emotional about it! You let that new car get a dent in it, you'll get emotional. You let your favorite ball team lose, you'll get emotional. You let that little child that is so dear to you get sick, you'll get emotional. When souls are important to you, you'll get emotional about it! We need to get our rejoicing in line with what heaven rejoices over. Heaven rejoices when a soul repents! Heaven gets happy when a person gets saved! We need to get our rejoicing and our excitement in line with what heaven gets excited about. This is the way I pray every time before I stand up and preach. I pray, "God, get me to preach in such a way that pleases Jesus and in such a way that Judy will rejoice." Heaven rejoices when souls get saved.

My oldest son, Brad, pastors in Augusta, Georgia at Abilene Baptist Church. Several years ago when he was still in seminary over in Memphis at the Mid-America Baptist Theological Seminary, he pastored a church in Hopewell, Tennessee. It was on Friday night about 11 o' clock and my phone rang. Just so you know, if you call me at 11 o' clock on a Friday night, you're going to wake me up. The phone woke me up, so I reached over and picked it up. I looked at the caller ID to see if I wanted to answer it or not. Don't act so surprised— you do the same thing. I saw it was Brad. I put it up to my face and said, "Boy, it better be important." He said, "Dad, it is important." I said, "What's going on?" He said, "This afternoon there was one of our young ladies, 34 years old, who just fell dead. We didn't know there was anything wrong with her. She just fell dead. She had a little son 5 years old named David and a daughter 7 years old named Amy. Dad, I have to preach her funeral this coming Monday. I don't know what to say. I don't know what to do." I said, "Brad, let's pray a while." That night over the phone we prayed together.

I waited until Monday evening when I knew everything would be over. I called Brad back and asked him, "Brad, how'd the funeral go?" He told me he'd never seen anything like it in his life. This lady was the daughter of a pastor in Memphis. She had a beautiful voice and she'd sung all over the mid-south area. Many of her songs had been recorded. They used her recordings for her music during the funeral. While they were playing recordings of her singing, someway, somehow, her little son David got lose from his father. He ran up to the casket and he could hear his mama's voice. He began to cry, "Mama, where you at?" He ran over to the speakers where he could hear her voice and said, "Mama, where you at? Mama, where you at?" Brad said it literally tore up that whole funeral service.

One of these days, little David is going to hear his mama's voice again. He'll know where she's at because he's going to be there with her. One of these days, I'm going to look into heaven. Literally, I'm going to look into heaven. You know why? Because I'm going to be there. If you're saved, one of these days you are going to literally, actually look into heaven because you're going to be there, too. Do you know that you know if you were to die in this very moment you would be with God in heaven? Will you look into heaven, too?

CHAPTER 6

WHAT HAPPENS IF YOU MISS THE RAPTURE?

If you will, open your Bible to Matthew 24:36-44. The Scripture says:

> *"But of that day and hour knoweth no man, no, not the angels of heaven, but My Father only. But as the days of Noah were, so shall also the coming of the Son of Man be. For as in the days that were before the flood they were eating and drinking, marrying and giving in marriage, until the day that Noah entered into the ark, and knew not until the flood came, and took them all away; so shall also the coming of the Son of Man be. Then shall two be in the field; the one shall be taken, and the other left. Two women shall be grinding at the mill; the one shall be taken, and the other left. Watch therefore: for ye know not what hour your Lord doth come. But know this, that if the goodman of the house had known in what watch the thief would come, he would have watched, and would not have suffered his house to be broken up. Therefore be ye also ready: for in such an hour as ye think not the Son of Man cometh."*

This Scripture is speaking about that great disappearing day. There's coming a day when the saved—the saints, the church—are going to be raptured out of this earth. I can imagine what the headlines of the newspapers will say the following day: "Christ returns. Millions missing around the world," or "Death stalks the highways." Cars will be running off the road. The policemen will not know what to do. Junk yards and impounds will be overflowing with empty cars. Cars will be running into each other because the driver has suddenly been taken up with God. I can imagine the headlines will read, "Fear grips the hearts of men." The Bible says in Luke 21:25-26:

> *"And there shall be signs in the sun, and in the moon, and in the stars; and upon the earth distress of nations, with perplexity; the sea and waves roaring; men's hearts failing them for fear, and for looking after those things which are coming on the earth: for the powers of heaven shall be shaken."*

Hospitals and morgues will be filled with people who died suddenly of a heart attack. I can imagine more of those little nitroglycerin pills will be sold than ever before. People will quickly be placing them under their tongues because they realize that their wife is missing, their husband is missing, their children are gone, their babies are gone. Godly preachers are gone. Those who love God are gone. This has gripped their hearts and they realize what has happened.

I believe the headlines will read, "Weeping mothers cry 'Where is my baby?'" Can you imagine a world with no babies? There's a hospital with a nurse carrying around a little newborn baby. Suddenly all she holds is air. There in the nursery at the hospital are empty cribs because all the babies have been taken. Then the headlines read, "Millions attempt suicide." The Bible says in Revelation 9:6, *"And in those days shall men seek death, and shall not find it; and shall desire to die, and death shall flee from them."* Can you imagine a world where people are trying to die and they can't? A man jumps off a bridge seeking to drown himself, but he cannot die. A person jumps off a ten-story building and his body hits the concrete and bursts open like an over-ripe melon, but he cannot die. Someone takes a gun, pulls the trigger, and tries to blow his brains out, but he cannot die. A person takes a needle and pumps that drug in his veins trying to kill himself with an overdose, but he cannot die. Men are going to seek death, and yet death will flee from them. We've heard a lot about the movie and the books *Left Behind*. What's going to happen if you're left behind?

You ask, "Pastor, when is the rapture going to take place?" Jesus said in Matthew 24:36, *"But of that day and hour knoweth no man, no, not the angels of heaven, but My Father only."* From time to time, you have someone who comes along and always wants to set a date. They have all the formulas and all the schemes about this certain date when Jesus is going to come back. You know what God said about that? They're stupid.

Even the angels in heaven don't know. In fact, Jesus said at that time He didn't even know. The Father only knows. We don't know when He may come back. He may well come back before this service is over. But mark it down: Jesus is coming again.

Now what's going to happen when Jesus comes? Let me share with you five events, you find in the book of Revelation that are going to take place when Jesus comes again.

1. THERE IS GOING TO BE RESURRECTION.

Revelation 20:6 says:

> *"Blessed and holy is he that hath part in the first resurrection: on such the second death hath no power, but they shall be priests of God and of Christ, and shall reign with Him a thousand years."*

There is a first resurrection and there is a second resurrection. Those who are going to be in the first resurrection are those who have been saved. The Bible says in I Thessalonians 4:16, *"The dead in Christ shall rise first."* There's going to be that great Getting Up Morning. There are some who say that when a Christian dies their spirit goes to be with the Lord and their body goes to the grave and will stay there forever and ever. Don't you buy that. He who quickened your spirit will one day quicken your body. It's true that when a Christian dies their spirit goes immediately into the presence of the Lord. Paul said to be absent from the body is to be present with the Lord. Jesus said to that dying thief, *"Today thou shalt be with Me in paradise."* When a Christian dies their spirit goes to be with the Lord immediately. Their body goes back to the dust of the earth to await the resurrection.

I heard about a man by the name of Mr. Peas who died. They put on his tombstone these words: "This ain't Peas. This is just the pod. Peas shelled out and went to be with God." One of these days, the One who took the spirit to be with Him is going to raise that body from the grave.

There will be people who died in Christ all across the face of the earth. Maybe they died at sea and their bodies are planted at the bottom of the sea. Maybe they've been cremated. Maybe their bodies lay in some remote cemetery in the jungles of Africa. On that glorious day, their bodies are going to come forth, their spirits are going to be reunited with their bodies, and they'll be given new bodies liken to His glorious body. The Bible says in I Corinthians 15:52, *"In a moment, in a twinkling of an eye, at the last trump: for the trumpet shall sound, and the dead shall be raised incorruptible, and we shall be changed."*

2. THERE IS GOING TO BE RAPTURE.

You see, we're not finished yet. We just talked about how the dead in Christ are raised first. What about those who are alive when Christ comes again? I fully expect to be alive when Jesus comes again. I may not be, but I expect to be. What's going to happen to those who are alive when Christ comes? Revelation 4:1 says:

"After this I looked, and, behold, a door was

opened in heaven: and the first voice which I heard was as it were of a trumpet talking with me; which said, Come up hither, and I will shew thee things which must be hereafter."

That reminds me of I Thessalonians 4:16-17 where it says:

"For the Lord Himself shall descend from heaven with a shout, with the voice of the archangel, and with the trump of God: and the dead in Christ shall rise first: then we which are alive and remain shall be caught up together with them in the clouds, to meet the Lord in the air: and so shall we ever be with the Lord."

That's where we get the word *rapture* from. We shall be raptured with them in the clouds to meet the Lord in the air and so shall we ever be with Him. It's going to be just like this: Jesus is going to come and He's going to come with a shout of the voice of the archangel and the trumpet of God. All those who are saved and alive are going to be called up immediately to go be with the Lord. If Jesus were to come in this very moment, I'd literally go through the roof to be with Him.

You say, "Don't you believe that's poetic language? Don't you believe that it should be taken symbolically?" No, I believe it literally. And I'll tell you why! There have been those who have been raptured literally before. Enoch was raptured. He was not for God took him. Elijah was raptured. The Bible says he was caught up in a whirlwind of fire. The people looked for him and asked, "Where is he? Where did he go?"

One of these days they're going to be looking for us. Where's the man who sat on the front row at church saying, "Amen" all the time? Where's the man who stood behind the pulpit and led in worship and praise? Where are those Christians who had a heart for God? Where are those preachers that loved God? Where are they? They'll try to surmise that some mysterious death ray was used. Oh, don't you believe it! Jesus has come. Can you imagine one of those big jets? The airlines think they're having problems now. All of a sudden that Christian pilot is taken. What's going to happen on those interstate highways? Won't be much different than they are now. All over this earth, Christians are going to be raptured.

3. THERE IS GOING TO BE RETRIBUTION.

This world is going rotten. This world spits in the face of God. This world tramples under its feet the precious blood of Jesus. Do you think that God will continue to let that take place? No! One of these days, the dam of God's mercy and grace will give way and His wrath will be poured out. There will be a Great Tribulation on this earth. If you're lost when Jesus comes, you'll be cast into that Great Tribulation. You can read in Scripture in Revelation 4 all the way through to Revelation 19:10, the Bible describes the Great Tribulation. What's going to take place? I can't go into great detail, but here are 5 statements about what will happen during the Great Tribulation.

- **THE WORLD WILL CONTINUE ON AFTER THE RAPTURE.** In fact, after the rapture this world will continue on 1,007 years. There will be seven years of Tribulation. Then there will be 1,000 years where the world just keeps turning. Some people believe there won't be 1,000 years after the rapture. They just believe there's a big Boom-Bang. That'd be it. The saved go to heaven; the lost go to hell. That's it. I was raised under preachers who we called amillennialists, which means "no millennium." I loved them. They were precious, but they were wrong. The Bible teaches that after the rapture, this world will continue on for 1,007 years. Yes, it's the end of the period of grace, but it isn't the end of the world.

- **THE CHURCH WILL NOT GO THROUGH THE TRIBULATION.** As you study through Scripture, you find during the Great Tribulation period, God deals with the Jews, the Gentiles, and the nations of the world. In no place do you find God dealing with the church here on the earth during the Great Tribulation. Revelation 1:19 says, *"Write the things which thou hast seen, and the things which are, and the things which shall be hereafter."* God is saying, "Now, John, I'm going to show you some things. Write these things."

  o *Write the things which thou hast seen.* That refers to Revelation 1 where John saw the vision of a glorified Christ.

o *The things which are.* That's Revelation 2-3. He speaks of the Church Age, the 7 churches.

o *The things that shall be hereafter.* That's in Revelation 4:1 all the way to the end of the book. So when you are at Revelation 4:1 and go forward, that's after the rapture. That's out there in the future. When you read through those chapters all the way through to Revelation 19:11, there is no mention of God dealing with the church on the earth. The Bible says in Revelation 19:11, *"And I saw heaven opened, and behold a white horse; and he that sat upon him was called Faithful and True, and in righteousness he doth judge and make war."*

The Bible talks about how He has the saints and the church come back with Him during that time. You see, the church does not go through the Tribulation. This is the way God always works. God always takes out His beloved before He pours out His wrath. That's the way He did with Lot. I know when you read about Lot, he doesn't always make godly decisions. You have to read all the way through the Old Testament and almost all the way through the New Testament to discover that Lot was just a man. But, he was a saved man. God took Lot out of Sodom and Gomorrah before He rained down fire and brimstone. Same thing was true of Noah. Before God sent the judgment flood, He first got Noah out and provided him an ark of safety. God takes His beloved out before He pours out His wrath! I thank God I'm not going to go through the Tribulation. If you want to go through it, then have at it. But friend, if you're saved, God is taking you out of this place.

- **THE ANTICHRIST WILL BE REVEALED DURING THE GREAT TRIBULATION.** Revelation 6:1-2 says:

    "And I saw when the Lamb opened one of the seals, and I heard, as it were the noise of thunder, one of the four beasts saying, Come and see. And I saw, and behold a white horse: and he that sat on him had a bow; and a crown was given unto him; and he went forth conquering, and to conquer."

Now, don't misinterpret that. That's not talking about Jesus. Here comes one with a bow. Do you see anything missing? An arrow. Here comes one—the Antichrist—without even firing a shot, without even having an arrow, and takes over through peace. He's going to have the idea that he's a great diplomat. Everyone is going to come forth and place themselves before him. The world is going to present to him all the military and the political and the economic power. What appears to be peace is actually the ushering in of Tribulation. This world rejected God's Christ, but they're going to accept the devil's christ. Jesus was the Lamb of God. The Antichrist is the devil's beast. Jesus was the Man of Sorrow. The Antichrist is the man of sin. Jesus is the Truth. The Antichrist is the lie. Jesus is the Holy One. The Antichrist is the wicked one. After the rapture of the church, the Antichrist is going to be revealed. A lot of times we speculate as to who the Antichrist might be. It may well be the Antichrist is alive and well on planet earth right now. Let me be real honest with you. If you're saved, he won't be revealed while we're here. It's only after the rapture of the church that he will come forth and his person and his nature will be revealed.

- **THE WRATH OF GOD WILL BE POURED OUT ON THIS EARTH DURING THE GREAT TRIBULATION.** The only thing that's keeping this earth from going rotten even more is the presence of Christians. As Christians, we are the salt of the earth. We are the light of the world. We live in a world where they mock and they ridicule Christians. You have your Jay Lenos, your David Lettermans, your Rosie O'Donalds. They always mock and ridicule Christians. Have you ever noticed the blunt end of all their jokes and all their laughter is the fundamental Christian—the Christian who wants to live and walk for God? We are the ridicule of their filthy minds. One of these days, they're going to discover the value of a real Christian. When that Christian is taken out of this world and then all restraints are taken off, this world is going to go totally rotten. Demons will come out of the bottomless pit and turn loose on this earth. The Bible says in Revelation 6:16-17:

> *"And said to the mountains and rocks, Fall on us, and hide us from the face of Him that sitteth on the throne, and from the wrath of the Lamb. For the great day of His wrath is come; and who shall be able to stand?"*

Notice they're not praying to the Lamb, but they're praying, *Hide us from the wrath of the Lamb* because judgment has come.

- **THERE WILL BE NO OPPORTUNITIES FOR YOU TO BE SAVED DURING THE GREAT TRIBULATION AFTER YOU REJECT CHRIST.** Some folks think, "Well Preacher, don't you think that after the church is taken out, people will look around and see what's taken place and they'll remember that sermon? Or they'll remember reading in the Bible and they'll realize what's taken place and then they'll come to Christ?" I've got an answer from the Bible. If you will not accept Christ during this age of grace, you will not accept Christ when judgment begins to fall. You may say, "Well, I always thought that there will be people who will be saved during the Tribulation." The Bible speaks about some who will come to the Messiah, but those are people who have never heard. You're not in that group.

118

You've heard. You're hearing right now, so that doesn't apply to you. Here is what applies to you in II Thessalonians 2:10-12:

> *"And with all deceivableness of unrighteousness in them that perish; because they received not the love of the truth, that they might be saved. And for this cause God shall send them strong delusion, that they should believe a lie: That they all might be damned who believed not the truth, but had pleasure in unrighteousness."*

In other words, they wouldn't be saved on a Sunday morning when they heard, "God loves you and Christ died for you. Come to Jesus!" They would not receive the love of the truth that they might be saved. Notice this next statement. *"And for this cause God will send them strong delusion, that they should believe a lie."* If you sit here today and you hear the Gospel and you say no to Jesus and Jesus were to come, you would be cast in the Great Tribulation. God will send you strong delusions and you're going to believe the lie. If you won't respond to His grace, you won't get saved when judgment begins to fall. If you're ever going to get saved, you need to come today. If you ever intend to come to Christ, you need to come today and be saved!

4. THE REIGN.

The next event of the calendar of God is the reign. Right

now, we're looking forward to the rapture. Then there will be 7 years where the lost will be cast in the Great Tribulation. All hell is going to break loose on this earth. The Antichrist is going to rule. At the end of that 7 years, Jesus will come and this time not for His church but with His church. There will be the battle of Armageddon and Jesus will be victorious! Then He will set up His kingdom on this earth and He will rule for 1,000 glorious years. In Revelation 20:1, the Bible says, *"And I saw an angel come down from heaven, having the key of the bottomless pit and a great chain in his hand."* There are those who are called amillenialists who say all this is symbolic. They say Satan has already been bound. If he's bound, he's on a long chain. Satan is alive and very active in the world today. If you've not already met him today and you're living for God, you'll meet him before the day is over. Continue reading in Revelation 20:

> *"And he laid hold on the dragon, that old serpent, which is the Devil, and Satan, and bound him a thousand years, and cast him into the bottomless pit, and shut him up, and set a seal upon him, that he should deceive the nations no more, till the thousand years should be fulfilled: and after that he must be loosed a little season. And I saw thrones, and they sat upon them, and judgment was given unto them: and I saw the souls of them that were beheaded for the witness of Jesus, and for the Word of God, and which had not*

worshipped the beast, neither his image, neither had received his mark upon their foreheads, or in their hands; and they lived and reigned with Christ a thousand years."

Jesus is going to come. He's going to set up His kingdom here. He's going rule and reign as King of Kings and Lord of Lords for 1,000 glorious years. There are those who say all this is symbolic. Well friend, if God did not mean what He said, then why didn't He say what He meant? He said for 1,000 years. This is going to be the golden age that philosophers have dreamed of through the ages. The curse of sin on this earth is going to be removed and He's going to rule and reign. We'll rule and reign with Him for 1,000 years.

5. READINESS.

Revelation 22:20 says, *"He which testifieth these things saith, Surely I come quickly. Amen. Even so, come, Lord Jesus."* When you got up this morning, did you think, "This may well be the day that Jesus comes"? Before your feet hit the floor, did you say, "This is the day Jesus is going to come"? If you didn't, that's one of the best proofs that this may well be the day. The Bible says here in Matthew 24:44, *"Therefore be ye also ready: for in such an hour as ye think not the Son of Man cometh."* When you least expect it, He's coming. Christian, are you ready for Jesus to come? You say, "Well, I thought all saved people are ready." I daresay that there's not a third of the Christians in the world that's really ready. I'm not talking about simply going to be with Jesus. First John 2:28 reads, *"And now, little children, abide in Him; that, when He shall appear, we may have confidence, and not be ashamed before Him at His coming."* If Jesus were to come right now, even if you're saved, many of you would want to crawl under your bed and hide because you've never led one soul to Christ. You'd have to go out and meet Him knowing you've got beer in your icebox. You know you have filthy magazines in your magazine racks. You know you've got God's tithe in your billfold. You've got hate in your heart. You're not ready for Jesus to come. Imagine a guy who's got a great big cigar in his mouth when Jesus comes. He's called up and for some reason God won't let him drop that cigar. All the way up to heaven he's trying to get rid of that thing. Are you ready for Jesus to come? First John 3:3 says, *"And every man that hath this hope in Him purifieth himself, even as He is pure."* If you really believe that Jesus is going to come any moment, it will cause you to walk the straight and narrow.

Lost friend, you're not ready for Jesus to come. The Bible says two will be in the field. One will be taken; one will be left. Two will be grinding at the mill. One will be taken; one will be left. Two will be in the bed. One will be taken; one will be left. Which one's going to be taken? The saved. Which one's going to be left? The lost.

Picture a wife who has such a burden and desire to see her husband come to Jesus. Early one morning Jesus comes and she's taken. The husband gets up and goes through his routine.

He showers and shaves and gets ready for the day. He walks into the kitchen thinking that, as always, his wife will have breakfast ready. The eggs are about burnt. He looks and he looks and he looks. But she's taken. He's been left behind.

See also a godly teenager who has a burden to see his unsaved mother come to Christ. Jesus comes one afternoon and he's taken. As always, she goes to pick him up at school. She sits and sits and sits, but he doesn't come. He's taken. She's left behind.

If Jesus were to come right now, would you be taken? If Christ were to come this very moment—and He may—would you be taken? Or would you be left behind?

CHAPTER 7

GETTING HOME BEFORE DARK

I heard about a preacher who, like myself, loves to hunt. He had gone hunting with one of his deacons one Saturday. The deacon had some young bird dogs he brought along with them. The pastor had carried with him that day his sermon notes that he was going to preach that next morning. Some way, somehow, one of the deacon's bird dogs got ahold of the pastor's sermon notes and ate some of them. However, the pastor was not aware of it. He got up that next Sunday morning and he opened up his Bible and began to preach. In about five minutes, he just stopped and closed his Bible then gave the invitation. After the service, there was a group of men that gathered around him and they said, "Pastor, what's the problem? Did you get sick? Was there something that happened?" He said, "No, not really. I went hunting yesterday with this deacon. Apparently, his bird dogs ate some of my sermon notes and that's all I had." I shared that with some of my own deacons and they said they were going to go look for some pups out of those bird dogs.

Jesus said in John 9:4, *"I must work the works of Him that sent Me, while it is day: the night cometh when no man can work."* Dr. Vance Havner was one of the greatest evangelists that was in Southern Baptist's life. He was also a great author. If you ever get an opportunity to read any of Dr. Havner's books, read them. He had a way of saying things that few men knew how to say. In one of his books, he tells the story about growing up as a boy in the mountains of North Carolina. He said that one of the things that his mother would always tell him when he left in the afternoon was, "Son, do the best you can to get home before dark." We say in a day like today that really doesn't make a great deal of sense to have a philosophy like that. For a boy growing up in the mountains of North Carolina over ninety years ago, that was good advice. He went on to say that it was his desire spiritually to make it home—that is, his heavenly home—before some darkness of sin overtook him and marred his life. I've thought a lot about that little statement: getting home before dark.

I want to share with you three men in the Bible who did not get home before dark. Realize, these were good men. These were noble men. These were Godly men. But the truth of the matter is they did not get home before dark.

1. NOAH DID NOT GET HOME BEFORE DARK BECAUSE HE WAS AN UNFAITHFUL PARENT.

Look back to Genesis 6:8-9, *"But Noah found grace in the eyes of the Lord."* By the way, that's the first time that you find the word *grace* in all the Bible. *"But Noah found grace in the eyes of the Lord. These are the generations of Noah: Noah was a just man and perfect in his generations and Noah walked with God."* What kind of man was Noah? We are told several things about him.

- **HE WAS A MAN OF CHARACTER.** The Bible says Noah was a just man. That word *just* is speaking about what he was on the inside. That word *just* is speaking about his inward stability and his moral purity. He was a man of character.

- **HE WAS A MAN OF CONSISTENCY.** The Bible says Noah was a just man and perfect in his generations. Now the word *perfect* does not mean what we think the word *perfect* means. When we think about a person being perfect, we think that means that they are without sin. However, we also understand that none of us are going to be perfect until we go to be with Jesus in glory one day. He was not a perfect man in the sense of being without sin. When the Bible says that he was a perfect man in his generations, it is talking about the consistency in his life. He was not up one day and down the next day. He was not hot one day and cold the next day. He was consistent.

- **HE WAS A MAN OF COMMUNION.** The Bible says that Noah was a just man and perfect in his generations and Noah walked with God. He knew what it was to have communion with God. When God created man then saw how man was living, God said, "I'm going to destroy man whom I have created." But the Bible says Noah found grace in the eyes of the Lord. The one person that God chose to speak forth the message of survival and salvation to that generation was Noah. Of all the people on the face of the earth, the one man that God chose to be His spokesman was Noah. What a privilege, what an honor! Why did God choose Noah? I'll tell you why. Noah walked with God.

- **HE WAS A MAN OF COMMITMENT.** He was committed to do whatever God told him to do. If you'll look over just another page to Genesis 7:5, the Bible says, *"and Noah did according unto all that the Lord commanded him."* When God gave him the instructions for building the ark, he obeyed God. He was committed to do it exactly the way God said to do it. God said build it so long and he built it so long. God said build it so wide and he built it so wide. God said build it so tall and he built it so tall. He was committed to do whatever God told him.

When you think of Noah, you think of someone who was a man of God. Of all the people God could have chosen, he chose Noah to be his spokesman to that generation. Noah and his family survived the flood. If the story ended right there, we would step back and applaud. We would say Noah made it home before dark, but that's not the end of the story.

The Bible tells us what happened after the flood was over. Genesis 9:20 says:

> *"And Noah began to be an husbandman, and he planted a vineyard: and he drank of the wine, and*

was drunken; and he was uncovered within his tent. And Ham, the father of Canaan, saw the nakedness of his father, and told his two brethren without. And Shem and Japheth took a garment, and laid it upon both their shoulders, and went backward, and covered the nakedness of their father; and their faces were backward, and they saw not their father's nakedness. And Noah awoke from his wine, and knew what his younger son had done unto him."

Look on down there to verses 28 and 29. The Bible says after that, *"Noah lived after the flood three hundred and fifty years. And all the days of Noah were nine hundred and fifty years: and he died."* What a tragic way for a man of God to die. Here's a man of character, consistency, communion, and commitment. Yet there he was, naked and drunk before his children. What a sad way for a man of God to end his life. Noah did not get home before dark because he was an unfaithful parent.

I could write a book about the unfaithful parents I have known through the years. There is a waywardness and a wickedness about the youth of America. I have a great burden for the young people of America. To be honest, our youth are facing things that you and I never faced in our day. The thing that amazes me more than the waywardness and the wickedness of the youth is the waywardness and the wickedness of parents in our day. Mothers and fathers ought to be living and setting an example for their children. I wonder what our young people must think when they see their mothers and their fathers trading wives and swapping husbands and getting drunk and living after the desires of the flesh. I wonder what they must think when they hear their parents say one thing with their mouth, then live a life of total contradiction.

If I know my own heart, I'd rather lay down and die than to have the time come when my boys would look back and say, "There was a day when our father lived for God but, in the latter days of his life, he turned his back on God." I would rather die right now than to have the time come and they say, "In the latter years of our father's life he became a disgrace to God." I don't want to live my life for God all the days, then be like Noah and have some moral indiscretion overtake me.

I dare say there are some of you who have set a good example for your children. You have built some stability, morality, and character into the lives of your children. Yet, in the last few months or years, the devil started to draw a circle around your life and he's just tempting you to chuck it all in and follow after the desires of the flesh. I've not read any of your mail and I've not listened to any of your phone calls. I'll guarantee you there are some couples that have already sat down and already decided that when your children move out of the house, when they go to college, you're going to get a divorce. You go your way; I'll go my way. Sir, madam, if you do that, the day will come when you'll stand before God and you'll hang your head in shame because you're going to realize that you didn't make it home before dark. If there's one way I want my boys to pray for me—not that God would bless me more, not even that God would help me to preach better sermons—it's that I'll finish with favor and I'll be true to the end. That ought to be the desire of every Christian parent.

2. MOSES DID NOT GET HOME BEFORE DARK BECAUSE HE WAS UNAWARE OF HIS POSITION.

Moses was an amazing man. The Bible tells us about Moses back in the book of Numbers 27:12-14:

> *"And the Lord said unto Moses, Get thee up into this mount Abarim, and see the land which I have given unto the children of Israel. And when thou hast seen it, thou also shalt be gathered unto thy people, as Aaron thy brother was gathered. For ye rebelled against my commandment in the desert of Zin, in the strife of the congregation, to sanctify me at the water before their eyes: that is the water of Meribah in Kadesh in the wilderness of Zin."*

No man knew power with God like Moses did. The hand of God was upon Moses from his very infancy. There were several times when God protected Moses and had His hand upon his life:

- When Pharaoh was killing the little baby boys.
- When Moses was reared in Pharaoh's palace.
- When the plagues came through the land.

130

- When Moses came to the Red Sea and the sea parted and he walked through on dry land.
- When God provided every need during the wilderness journeys.
- When Moses went up on the mountain and God gave him the ten commandments.
- When Moses came face to face with the glory of God.

No man saw the things Moses saw. No man knew the power of God like Moses did. If the story ended right there, we would step back and we would applaud and we would say Moses made it home before dark. But that's not the end of the story.

You'll remember God took Moses to the mount and He said to Moses, "Moses, you can look into the land, but you're not going to enter into the land. Moses, you can look into Canaan, you can look into the Promised Land, but you're not going to walk in the land. In fact, Moses, you're going to die ahead of time." Why didn't God allow Moses to enter into the Promised Land? In fact, why did God kill Moses? If you look to Numbers 20:7 and on, the Bible says, *"And the Lord spake unto Moses, saying, take the rod..."* This is the same rod that was a symbol of the miracle-working power of God. It's the same rod Moses lifted over the Red Sea where the sea parted. It's the same rod where, on another occasion, God told Moses to strike a rock and water came forth. Another time Moses stood on the mountain with the rod of God and the valley down below. When Moses lowered the rod of God, there was defeat in the valley.

When he raised the rod of God, there was victory in the valley. It was a symbol of the miracle-working power of God. Let's continue reading. God said:

"Take the rod, and gather thou the assembly together, thou, and Aaron thy brother, and speak ye unto the rock before their eyes; and it shall give forth to them water out of the rock: so thou shalt give the congregation and their beasts drink. And Moses took the rod from before the Lord, as he commanded him. And Moses and Aaron gathered the congregation together before the rock, and he said unto them, Hear now, ye rebels; must we fetch you water out of this rock? And Moses lifted up his hand, and with his rod he smote the rock twice: and the water came out abundantly, and the congregation drank, and their beasts also. And the LORD spake unto Moses and Aaron, Because ye believed Me not, to sanctify Me in the eyes of the children of Israel, therefore ye shall not bring this congregation into the land which I have given them. This is the water of Meribah; because the children of Israel strove with the Lord, and he was sanctified in them."

What caused God to take this drastic action? Why did God take the life of Moses? I'll tell you why: Moses was unaware of his position. Up to this point, whenever there was a miracle of God, it was always obvious that God was doing it and that Moses was merely the human instrument through which God was working. Moses gave God the glory. But here, in presumptuous pride, Moses stands up before the children of Israel, and he cries, *"Here now ye rebels. Must we fetch you water out of this rock?"* He began to take the credit himself which was to be given unto God. He began to magnify himself.

I'm convinced there are a lot of folks who will not make it home before dark because they begin to magnify themselves. You and I could name preacher after preacher. We all have known of nationally famous evangelists or pastors who, at one time, had the hand of God upon them, but they began to magnify themselves. They got the idea that, "I'm bigger than God." Today they are out of ministry altogether. They became a disgrace to God, their church, and their families. I could name deacon after deacon that I've known through the years—real men of God—who got the idea, "It's my church; I'm the boss and I call the shots." Before long, they were totally washed out and they turned their backs on God. I'm sure we could all name people God blessed with abilities to preach, sing, teach, or minister in some way. But they got the idea that God couldn't do it without them. They thought, "I'm the one that's really doing this." Before long, they're totally washed out in their walk with God. The truth is, though, I'm nothing. You're nothing. If there's anything good in me, or if there's anything good in you, it's because of the blessed Lord Jesus who lives within us. I'm just a zero with the edges rubbed out. I'm nothing. But I want to tell you, He's everything! He's awesome!

Let me describe to you in New Testament terminology what happened to Moses. Moses committed the sin unto death. The Bible says, "to much was given, much shall be required." God blessed Moses with much and God expected much from Moses. The Bible says in 1 John 5:16, *"If any man see his brother sin a sin which is not unto death,* [Now, the only way a person can be your brother spiritually is if he is saved. This is speaking about a Christian. This is not speaking to a lost person.] *he shall ask, and he shall give him life for them that sin not unto death. There is a sin unto death: I do not say that he shall pray for it."*

The sin unto death is a sin which a Christian commits. Moses was a child of God. As we would say, Moses was a Christian. The sin of death is when a Christian crosses God's deadline and God takes their life physically. Yes, they're saved and, if you're saved, you go to heaven when you die. You have everlasting, eternal life. However, God takes you to heaven prematurely because He does not want to leave you here to bring embarrassment upon His name.

For example, my youngest son, Paul, was a student at Union University in Jackson, Tennessee. Let's just suppose, hypothetically, one night Paul was arrested for the possession and the use of an illegal drug. The next morning in the Jackson

Sun newspaper, it would not report Paul Whitt, student at Union University, was arrested for the use and possession of an illegal drug. It would say, "The son of a Baptist evangelist was arrested for the possession and use of an illegal drug." You see, what my son does is a reflection upon me. What we do as Christians is a reflection upon the Father. The Father has every right to protect His integrity any way He can.

Here's another illustration. In I Corinthians 5:1, Paul is writing to the church at Corinth:

> *"It is reported commonly that there is fornication among you, and such fornication as is not so much as named among the Gentiles, that one should have his father's wife."*

Apparently, here was a young man who was living in an immoral relationship with his step-mother, his father's wife. And then Paul said in verse 5, *"to deliver such an one unto Satan for the destruction of the flesh, that the spirit may be saved in the day of the Lord Jesus."* In other words, he says to turn him over to Satan for the destruction of the flesh, a physical death, that his spirit may be saved in the day of the Lord Jesus. Yes, he goes to heaven but he goes to heaven prematurely. When God saves us, He convicts us when we do wrong, when we sin. When you're saved, you can't get by with your sin. When you sin as a Christian, there's going to be an alarm going off in your heart, in your spirit, to let you know what you're doing is wrong. There will be conviction. If you continue on in that sin, God will chasten you; that is, God will spank or discipline you. The Bible says that if any be without chastisement, then you are illegitimate. You're not real sons and daughters. You're not saved. How many of you have ever been spanked by God? After God has convicted you then chastened you, if you continue on in that sin, there may well come a day then God will say, "That's it," and He'll take your life physically. Sure, you go to heaven, but you go there ahead of time. He says, "Satan, take his life. Kill him," and you die in the devil's slaughterhouse.

You probably wonder, "Preacher, have you ever seen that happen?" I believe I have. Several years ago I went to pastor a church in Athens, Tennessee. I was just 27 years old and this church had been without a pastor for a year and a half. They had gone through a church split. They'd had a Baptist fight. God have mercy on churches that fuss and fight. They literally ran the pastor off. They talked to me about going to be their pastor. To be honest with you, I didn't want to go there. I was convinced God wanted me to go there, but I went with fear and trembling. Let me hasten to say that five of the best years of my life were spent at that church. That place became a wonderful, loving, gracious place and we loved it. But there was a man in our church who at one time was a Sunday School teacher, a deacon, chairman of the deacons, and a trustee. At one point he was even the treasurer. Some way, somehow, he got hurt. He was injured through all the fussing and fighting at the church.

One evening, my next door neighbor came over to my house about suppertime and he knocked on the door. He said, "Pastor, I want you to make a visit with me tonight." I said, "Well, let me finish my meal and we'll go." After I finished eating, we rode over to see the man who had gotten hurt. We got out of the car, walked up and knocked on the door. Pretty soon afterward, he came to the door. I'd never met him before that time. My church member introduced me to him and he graciously invited us in. We went in, sat down, and had a pleasant conversation about family, life, and so on.

Finally, I knew it was time to get around to why we visited. I looked at him and said, "I understand there was a day that God was real in your life and He used you in a great way. But some way, somehow, you were hurt, you were injured, and you have dropped out of church." I said, "I want to appeal to you. I want to plead with you to come back to God. Whether you ever come back to the church I pastor, that's not the issue. I want to plead with you to come back to God and start living for Him again." I'll never forget how the countenance changed on his face. That man gritted his teeth and he clenched his fists and he pounded his knees. He said, "I'll never come back. I'll never come back to that church. I'll never come back to God." When he made that statement, almost before I knew what I was saying, the following words came out of my mouth. I've never said them to a person before nor since. I looked at him and said, "God's going to kill you." We just stood up, walked out of the house.

When we got in the car, my neighbor said to me, "Brother, do you realize what you just said to that man?" I said, "I'm afraid I do." Less than three weeks passed before that man fell dead of a heart attack. I will never forget as I stood there at that open grave. It was almost like God just said, "There's a man that I killed. He crossed over the line."

If you're saved and you know you have unconfessed sin in your life, you're on dangerous ground. It may be bitterness, malice, jealousy, or actual sexual sin. I don't care what it may be. Friend, you're on dangerous ground. You may be a lot closer to death than you realize. I pray to God that there won't be some untimely funerals in the near future.

I don't want to go home in the dark. Do you? I don't want to die in the devil's slaughterhouse. When it comes time for old Don to die, I want Him to send the gentlest angel He's got in heaven after me. I want to go home in the light. I want to be true. I want to be faithful to the very end. It may well be that God has already taken someone's death warrant out. He's got His pen poised and He's waiting to see what you're going to do in a few moments. If you harden your neck and harden your heart and say, "No, I won't do it," God just might sign your death warrant. Don't bother calling the pastor to come and pray for you then. It'll be too late. Don't bother calling the deacons to come and pray for you then. It'll be too late. If I knew I was saved but I knew there was unconfessed sin in my life, I wouldn't wait. I'd fall on my face and call out to God to have mercy upon me.

3. DAVID DID NOT GET HOME BEFORE DARK BECAUSE OF UNRESTRAINED PASSIONS.

David just appeared out of nowhere on the pages of the Bible. The prophet Samuel came to David's father, Jesse, to find and anoint the next king over Israel. Jesse had all of his big fine sons stand in front of Samuel. Samuel said, "Not this one, not this one, not this one, not this one." Finally, Samuel looked at Jesse and said, "Don't you have any more sons?" Jesse said, "Well, I've got a little son who's taking care of the sheep out in the field." Samuel said, "Send for him. Bring him in." David came there and the prophet said, "This is him." He anointed David the next king over Israel.

God was so real in David's life. He fought against Goliath and, with one smooth stone, he killed the giant. With his bare hands, he killed the lion and the bear. He led the Israelites into battle and had victory over the Philistines. No man loved God the way David loved God. The Bible says David was a man after God's own heart. If the story ended right there, we would step back and we would applaud and we would say, "David made it home before dark." But that's not the end of the story.

Do you remember how David began to grow in power and might? On one occasion, the army was out fighting the battle but David stayed back. He looked over at a neighbor's wife and lusted after her while she bathed. David sent for her and he committed adultery with her. After he committed that sin of adultery, he covered it up by murdering her husband. When the prophet Nathan came to David in II Samuel 12:7, he said:

> *"Thou art the man. Thus saith the Lord God of Israel, I anointed thee king over Israel, and I delivered thee out of the hand of Saul; And I gave thee thy master's house, and thy master's wives into thy bosom, and gave thee the house of Israel and of Judah; and if that had been too little, I would moreover have given unto thee such and such things. Wherefore hast thou despised the commandment of the Lord, to do evil in His sight? thou hast killed Uriah the Hittite with the sword, and hast taken his wife to be thy wife, and hast slain him with the sword of the children of Ammon. Now therefore the sword shall never depart from thine house; because thou hast despised me, and hast taken the wife of Uriah the Hittite to be thy wife. Thus saith the Lord, Behold, I will raise up evil against thee out of thine own house, and I will take thy wives before thine eyes, and give them unto thy neighbour, and he shall lie with thy wives in the sight of this sun. For thou didst it secretly: but I will do this thing before all Israel, and before the sun."*

He said, "Now, David, you did this thing in secret but I'm going to reveal it to the whole world." Some of you men go off on a business trip and you have some woman meet you there who's not your wife. Some of you ladies have some man come by your house when your husband's at work. Some of you young people go out on a date and in the back seat of the car you take liberties with your hands that you have no business taking. You think no one will ever know about it. God knows. One day, God's going to broadcast it to all the world. David said, "I have sinned against the Lord." Nathan said in essence, "David, God's not going to take your life. God has forgiven you of your sin and you're going to live."

Don't say amen too quickly because the story's not over yet. If you look further down in 2 Samuel 12:15, there's one of the most awesome statements in all of the Bible. *"And Nathan departed unto his house. And the Lord struck the child that Uriah's wife bare unto David, and it was very sick."* I don't understand all that's involved in that statement. I've had people argue with me and say that the Lord will never strike a child because of the parent's sin. Let me ask you a question. Did God ever do it once? The Bible says there, *"and the Lord struck the child."* I don't understand all of it but I do know this: God has not changed. God is the same yesterday, today, and forever. I'm a father and I don't want to do anything in my life that might cause the Lord to strike down one of my three boys.

There are some of you who know there's sin in your life. You know it, but you say in your heart, "I don't care what that preacher says. I don't care what God says. I don't care what the

Bible says. I'm going to live the way I want to live and no one is going to change me." There may come that day when you'll get that phone call in the middle of the night, three or four o'clock in the morning, and it's the police station. They say, "Come quickly to the emergency room. Your son or your daughter's been in a terrible accident." You make your way there to the emergency room and you meet the doctor. The doctor says, "Your son, your daughter's been in a terrible accident and we don't know if they're going to live." You walk back out there to that emergency room and you get down on that old concrete floor. You begin to cry out and you say, "God, forgive me of my sin. God, forgive me of my sin. God, don't let my boy die. Don't let my girl die. God, let them live. Let them live!" There's going to be that still, small voice that's going to speak to your heart. He's going to say, "Do you know why your son or your daughter's in there? You loved your sin more than you loved Me. It was the only way I could get your attention." I don't know what you think about your sin right now, but I can tell you this much, God hates your sin. God hates my sin. God hates our sin so much that He allowed His Son Jesus to go on the cross and die that we might get forgiveness of sin. What is it going to take for you to get right with God? Are you going to be like Noah, an unfaithful parent? Moses, unaware of your position? David, unrestrained in your passions? What's it going to take for you to get right with God?

Anyone who knows about sports in America recognizes the name of Woody Hayes. He was the coach at Ohio State University in Columbus, Ohio. This coach won over 200 collegiate victories and a national championship. Do you remember that day when Ohio State played Clemson in the Bowl Game? I remember it. I will never forget. Ohio State was marching down the field to a certain victory. A pass was made, but it was intercepted by a Clemson player and the Clemson player started running back down the field. I could hardly believe my eyes. The Ohio State coach, Woody Hayes, ran out, grabbed that Clemson player by the face mask and socked him right in the face. Nobody could believe what they saw. The next morning, Woody Hayes resigned in disgrace. Now when you think of Woody Hayes across America, you don't think about the 200 victories. You don't think about the national championship. But you do remember that one event that marred his career and his life.

I don't know about you. I don't want to allow sin to mar my life and not make it home before dark. I want to be clean. I want to be pure. I want to be faithful to the very end. Don't you want to make it home before dark?

CHAPTER 8

MAGNIFY THE NAME OF JESUS

Three times in Acts 19 you find the phrase "the name of the Lord Jesus." The first time is in verse 5. The Scripture says this, *"when they heard this, they were baptized in the name of the Lord Jesus."* That is in reference to the confession of the name of the Lord Jesus. Then the second reference is down in verse 13:

> *"Then certain of the vagabond Jews, exorcists, took upon them to call over them which had evil spirits the name of the Lord Jesus, saying, We adjure you by Jesus whom Paul preacheth."*

That is a reference to the power of the name of the Lord Jesus. The third reference is down in verse 17. *"And this was known to all the Jews and Greeks also dwelling in Ephesus; and fear fell on them all, and the name of the Lord Jesus was magnified."* That is a reference to the glorifying of the name of the Lord Jesus. It is this third reference that I want to build the message around where the Bible says, *"And fear fell on them all, and the name of the Lord Jesus was magnified."*

Doctor Luke, who was the human author of the book of Acts, tells us there were certain things that happened at Ephesus as the result of the Apostle Paul being there. Among the many things that took place, one thing in particular that happened was that the name of the Lord Jesus was magnified. The name of the Lord Jesus was made larger. The name of the Lord Jesus grew. I remember when I was a boy there were many times in the hot summer when I would go outside. I'd take a magnifying glass and a piece of paper to magnify those sun rays through the glass onto the paper in just the right way. When the sun rays were magnified on that paper in the right way, all of a sudden the piece of paper would burst into flames. That's the idea here. The name of the Lord Jesus was magnified.

Those of us who wear glasses understand a little something about this. I didn't wear glasses until I was about 40 years old. Judy, my wife, came up to me and said, "You need to go get your eyes examined." I asked, "Why?" She said, "Every time you stand up and read the Bible, you're embarrassing me." I said, "What do you mean, I'm embarrassing you?" She said, "You're just calling words everything." I replied, "I knew I was having a little difficulty. I just thought if I got the Bible far enough out there, I could get it right or I'd just sort of guess at it." She said, "Well, you're guessing wrong!" We're not going to guess anymore. We're going to see how the name of the Lord Jesus was magnified.

When Paul came to Ephesus, there were things that he did that magnified the name of the Lord Jesus. I believe God is saying this should be the desire of our hearts. The question we should ask is this: what is it that magnifies His name? Here are five things we find in Acts 19 on how to do just that.

1. THE NAME OF THE LORD JESUS IS MAGNIFIED BY A CONFIDENT MESSAGE.

Let's read Acts 19:1-5 together:

> *"And it came to pass, that, while Apollos was at Corinth, Paul having passed through the upper coasts came to Ephesus: and finding certain disciples, he said unto them, Have ye received the Holy Ghost since ye believed? And they said unto him, We have not so much as heard whether there is any Holy Ghost. And he said unto them, Unto what then were ye baptized? And they said, Unto John's baptism. Then said Paul, John verily baptized with the baptism of repentance, saying unto the people, that they should believe on Him which should come after him, that is, on Christ Jesus. When they heard this, they were baptized in the name of the Lord Jesus."*

When Paul came to Ephesus, he found a small group of 12 disciples. These were 12 disciples of John the Baptist who were baptized by John's baptism. They'd gone as far as John, but they had not made it to Jesus in real salvation. So in the true New Testament sense, they were not Christians. Paul discovered this by asking them some questions. He asked them, "When you believed, did you receive the Holy Spirit? When you believed, did you just believe certain things in your mind, or did you receive a new life?" He asked, "What took place?" They replied,

146

"We've not even heard if there is a Holy Spirit or not." Then he asked them another question, "Under what baptism were you baptized?" They said, "Under John's baptism." Paul said then, "John baptized with a baptism of repentance saying to the people that they should believe on Him who should come after him, that is, on Christ Jesus." The Bible says that when they heard this, they were baptized in the name of the Lord Jesus. I believe what that means is this: Paul went on and explained to them the way of real salvation. He preached to them the Gospel of Christ. He preached to them Christ died according to the Scriptures, Christ was buried according to the Scriptures, Christ arose according to the Scriptures, and Christ was exalted according to the Scriptures. All who would repent of their sins and believe in Christ would be born into the family of God. One thing that magnifies the name of the Lord Jesus is the clear, simple preaching of the Gospel of Christ.

There are a lot of people who might say, "Well, preaching has had its day. Preaching is ol' fogy. We have to replace it with a dialogue or a monologue. Preaching is dead." Now, there's a lot of dead preaching and there's a lot of dead preachers, but preaching is not dead. The greatest thing that takes place week in and week out across this land is when the men of God—the called of God, the anointed of God—stand up and preach the Word of God!

I realize a lot of times preachers are strange. I was out hunting one day. Truthfully, I was in camouflage and I had my old pickup truck and my old dogs. No one would have ever guessed I was a preacher. I stopped in to an old country store to get a big, thick sandwich for lunch. I didn't think anyone would have any idea who I was. When I walked in that store, there was a young man who was about 17 or 18 years old. He looked over at me and said, "You're a preacher, ain't you?" I said, "Yes, but why do you say that?" He said, "I can spot 'em a mile away." The good news is that I shared the Gospel with him and led him to Christ right there in that country store. The Bible says in I Corinthians 1:21, *"It pleased God by the foolishness of preaching to save them that believe."*

Wherever Paul went, he preached the Gospel of Christ. In Romans 10:13-15, Paul said:

> *"For whosoever shall call upon the name of the Lord shall be saved. How then shall they call on Him in whom they have not believed? And how shall they believe in Him of whom they have not heard? And how shall they hear without a preacher? And how shall they preach, except they be sent? As it is written, How beautiful are the feet of them that preach the Gospel of peace, and bring glad tidings of good things!"*

Paul went on to say in I Corinthians 2:2, *"I am determined to not know any thing among you, save Jesus Christ, and Him crucified."* Paul said, "I am determined that wherever I go, I'm going to preach the clear, simple Gospel of Christ." It didn't matter if he was in the palace or the prison. It didn't matter whether he was in the market place or the high sea. Wherever Paul was he lifted high the crucified, the risen, the exalted, the soon-coming Lord Jesus Christ. One thing that magnifies the name of the Lord Jesus is the preaching of the Word of God.

The man who does that preaching may not always use the King's English in the proper way. He may not always know the latest techniques of sermon delivery and preparation. But if that man is called of God, anointed of God, and he's telling people that by repenting of sin and trusting in Jesus they can be saved whenever and wherever that takes place, the name of the Lord Jesus is magnified. I'm not interested in you ever leaving your church saying, "Good sermon." I want you to leave saying, "Jesus is an awesome, mighty Savior!"

2. THE NAME OF THE LORD JESUS IS MAGNIFIED BY A CONVERTED MEMBERSHIP.

Were these 12 disciples of John Christians or not? Were they saved or not? When you read verse 2 in the King James, it almost seems to be speaking of some kind of second blessing. The Bible says, *"He said unto them, have you received the Holy Ghost since you believed? And they said unto him, we have not so much as heard whether there be any Holy Ghost."* But if you read in other translations—and I believe they're translated correctly—it is translated this way: when you believed, did you receive the Holy Spirit? You never build a major doctrine on one verse. All of Scripture will dove-tail together; it will never contradict. When you read this in the King James, it almost seems to indicate that he's speaking about something that takes place after salvation. In reality, he's talking about something that takes place at the very moment of salvation. I've changed my understanding of that passage through the years. I used to read that and think, "Well, perhaps that was saying they had entered into a fullness of the Spirit or a deeper walk with God." After reading that and looking at the rest of the Word of God, I've come under conviction that these disciples were not saved at all. You cannot be saved unless you have the Holy Spirit.

- *"But ye are not in the flesh, but in the Spirit, if so be that the Spirit of God dwell in you. Now if any man have not the Spirit of Christ, he is none of his."* – Romans 8:9
- *"For by one Spirit are we all baptized into one body, whether we be Jews or Gentiles, whether we be bond or free; and have been all made to drink into one Spirit."* – I Corinthians 12:13

That is, if you're saved, you have been baptized by the Spirit of God into the body of Christ. That took place at the very moment of salvation.

Sometimes I get into a rocking, weaving way when I preach. I was preaching at a revival sometime back. After the service was over, I had someone come up to me and say, "You've got it, ain't you?" I asked, "Got what?" He said, "You've got the Holy Ghost." I said, "You better believe it!" When I said that, I wasn't saying what he thought I was saying. What I was saying

150

was that when I was a 13-year old boy in Vacation Bible School, Jesus saved me and I got the Holy Ghost. The Spirit of God came to live within my heart and I was baptized into the body of Christ in that very moment. The question is not so much do you have the Holy Spirit, but does the Holy Spirit have you?

These disciples were not real Christians. They were moral people. They were good people. They made it to John, but they hadn't made it to Jesus. I'm convinced there are a lot of folks like that in the church today. You've joined the church, you've been baptized, you've walked down a church aisle but you've never made it to Jesus. It's one thing to get your name on a church row; it's quite a different thing to get your name in the Lamb's Book of Life.

Gypsy Smith was a great evangelist, but also he was a gypsy. On one occasion, he was meeting with a band of gypsies. There was a lady there who looked out of place. He made his way over to her and asked her, "Ma'am, are you a gypsy?" She said, "yes." He wasn't satisfied. He made his way back to her a little later and asked, "Are you certain that you're a gypsy?" She said, "I told you, I am a gypsy!" Finally, he went back a third time. He said, "Ma'am, I don't mean to insult you, but are you really a gypsy?" She looked back at him and said, "I can't fool you. I just joined!"

I'm convinced there are a lot of folks like that today. They really don't have Jesus. All they've done is joined the church. I believe Billy Graham indeed is correct when he said the greatest mission field in America are the church rolls of America. One thing I've noticed particularly over the last few years, as I preached crusades and revivals, is that church members, religious people are coming and saying, "I've never really been saved, and I need to be saved."

Several years ago I was pastor of North Athens Church in Athens, Tennessee. One Sunday night one of our deacons, Gene Pierman, came to me during the invitation, took me by the hand and said, "Pastor, I want to come tonight and openly and publicly confess that I trusted Jesus as my Savior today and I need to follow the Lord in believer's baptism." You know how we pastors normally do. I said, "Now, Gene, what you're saying is that you've made a deeper commitment to God and you want to walk with God and you want to live for God." He said, "No Pastor, I got saved this afternoon. This afternoon at 2 o' clock, I made my way here to this altar by myself, got on my knees, repented of my sins and asked Jesus to save me and He saved me!" I said, "Gene, tell me what's been happening?" He said, "Barbara [his wife] and I got married when we were just older teenagers. We had no church background whatsoever. We'd been married about 6 months when a preacher came by on a Saturday morning. He knocked on our door and then came in. He looked over at me and said, 'Gene, wouldn't you like to become a Christian?' Anyone with good sense would like to become a Christian. I said, 'Of course!' The preacher said, 'I'm going to pray for you that you'll become a Christian.' That man knelt beside my couch and I knelt beside him. He prayed for me. I didn't pray anything; I just listened to him pray. We stood up, the preacher took me by the hand, and he said, 'Now you're a Christian.' I didn't know any different."

Gene went on to explain how the next morning he went forward and told the church he became a Christian. He got baptized and got active in church. He really wanted to please God. He started working in Sunday School. They were running a bus at the church, so Gene became a bus captain. Later Gene was ordained as a deacon. Someway, somehow, Gene realized something was missing. Every time there was a revival, Gene came forward and rededicated his life again and again. He soon came to realize you can't rededicate something that was never dedicated in the first place. Gene said, "I came to the point where I just couldn't go on any longer. This afternoon, I got it settled and Jesus saved me!"

I wonder if there are some of you like that. You've walked down some church aisle. You took a preacher by the hand. You nodded your head to a few questions. You went under the water of baptism. You've been active in church membership. You try to live by the ten commandments. You try to live by the golden rule. You try to do all those things, but somewhere, someway, you've missed Jesus. If that's your condition, you need to give your heart to Christ! You ask, "What will people say?" Doesn't matter. You ask, "What will people think?" Doesn't matter! Heaven's too sweet, hell's too hot, and eternity's too long to be wrong about Jesus! When religious people, when church members get supernaturally converted by the Holy Ghost, the name of the Lord Jesus is magnified!

3. **THE NAME OF THE LORD JESUS IS MAGNIFIED BY A CLEAR MANDATE.**

When God's word is obeyed, the name of Jesus is magnified. What is the first command God gives after we're saved? Matthew 28:18-19 says:

> *"Jesus came and spake to them, saying, All power is given unto Me in heaven and in earth. Go ye therefore, and teach all nations* [that is, go and win people], *baptizing them in the name of the Father, and of the Son, and of the Holy Ghost."*

What's the first thing that's to take place after you're saved? You're to follow the Lord in believer's baptism. Acts 19:5 says, *"When they heard this* [that is, when they heard the Gospel], *then they were baptized in the name of the Lord Jesus."* I wonder if Paul said, "Now that you've been saved, I want you to think about being baptized. I want you to pray about being baptized." Do you think that's what Paul said? No, that's what we say. I believe Paul really looked over to them and said, "Now since you've been saved, I'm going to tell you what Jesus said. You need to be baptized!" You say, "What's the big compulsion about baptism?" Let me make this very clear. Water baptism does not save. You can get baptized in every pond, every creek, and every river in America so many times that the fish and

154

tadpoles know your social security number frontwards and backwards. If that's all that happens, all that took place was that you went down a dry sinner and came up a wet sinner. That water will not save you. Only the blood of Jesus saves. Baptism is not essential for salvation, but baptism is essential for obedience. You'll never go on in your walk with God until you obey that first command to be baptized as a believer.

I wonder about people who say they're saved but they won't be baptized. Folks, that's just water. The big question is the blood. If you trusted Jesus, then the big question has been settled. Follow on and do what God has told you to do. When a person is baptized as a believer, as they're placed under the water and lifted out of the water, they're saying, "I died to an old life, I've been given a new life in Jesus!" It may be that some of you, back yonder somewhere, had some kind of experience and you went through some kind of baptism, but later you've really been saved. You need to obey Jesus and be baptized as a believer. You see, when a person obeys that command to be baptized as a believer, the name of the Lord Jesus is magnified.

4. THE NAME OF THE LORD JESUS IS MAGNIFIED BY A CONQUERED MENACE.

When the powers of the devil are torn down by the power of God, the name of the Lord Jesus is magnified. Look down at Acts 19:13:

> *"Then certain of the vagabond Jews, exorcists, took upon them to call over them which had evil*

spirits the name of the Lord Jesus saying, We adjure you by Jesus whom Paul preacheth. And there were seven sons of one Sceva, a Jew, and chief of the priests, which did so. And the evil spirit answered and said, Jesus I know, and Paul I know; but who are ye?"

Let me pause and say this, Paul was known in hell. Are you known in hell? He said, "Jesus I know, Paul I know, but who are you?" You ought to be known in hell! You ought to cause hell trouble! Does hell tremble because of your dedication and your devotion to God?

Continue to read on there. *"And the man in whom the evil spirit was leaped on them, and overcame them, and prevailed against them, so that they fled out of that house naked and wounded."* Here were these Satan-inspired Jews who were trying to use the name of Jesus as some kind of lucky rabbit's foot. God would not allow that. That man, possessed by the evil spirit, leaped on them. The Bible says they ran out of that house naked and wounded. Contrary to popular belief, Satan is not dead. Satan is not a figment of our imagination. Satan is alive in the world today. Demons are active in the world today. If I had time, I'd share with you how over the last few years, I've seen more demonic activity than I have in all my life. I'm not one to see a demon behind every bush, but I want you to know that the devil and demons are real in the world today. I want to tell you also, although we do not have the power in and of ourselves over

Satan and demons, I know One who does. Greater is He who is in you than he who is in the world. You see, when the power of Jesus comes against the power of the devil, the hell holes and the Satan dens have to go!

Wouldn't you love to see the power of God come over your hometown in real revival power? What happens when revival breaks out in a city? Things are different! The beer joints begin to close down. The X-rated, R-rated movies have no one going to them. The places peddling their pornography will have no one going and buying their goods. The abortion clinics will have to close their doors! When God comes on a place, things are different!

I just want to share my heart with you for a moment. Please hear me. I don't want to live my life and die and just talk about what God used to do or how He used to move in revival. I don't want to live and die and just talk about how God moved in revival on Mount Carmel with Elijah, what He did on Pentecost with Peter; what God used to do during the Great Awakening with the Wesleys, the Whitfields, and the Billy Sundays; or what He used to do during the early 1950s when Billy Graham preached crusades across America. Friend, I want to see God do great and mighty things today! If all we do is talk about what God used to do in the past, then we might as well shut down the shop and say, "That's it." But what God did in the past God is still mighty to do today.

My prayer is that God will just sit down where you are

and move in revival power. Jesus has the power to set the captive free. Maybe you're still chained with sin. You're bound with lust. You're bound with discouragement. You're chained with depression. I want to tell you the Lord Jesus can set you free. When the power of God comes on a place and the power of Satan is defeated, the name of the Lord Jesus is magnified.

5. THE NAME OF THE LORD JESUS IS MAGNIFIED BY CLEAN MEN.

The Bible says in Acts 19:18, *"And many that believed came, and confessed, and shewed their deeds."* They didn't just walk down an aisle and join a church. They came and believed and confessed and it was revealed by their deeds, their lifestyle. Their lives were different. When they went home, they were different. When they went to school, they were different. When they went to work, they were different. They used to be drunks; now they're sober. They used to be liars; now they're truth tellers. They used to curse; now they praise. Jesus makes you different!

I had someone tell me a while back, "Brother Don, don't go out and tell people that when you become a Christian, things immediately change." I said, "Where'd you get that? The Bible says, 'therefore if any man be in Christ, he is a new creature. Old things have passed away, behold, all things become new.'" Now, we're not perfect yet. We're not going to be perfect until we go to be with Jesus in glory. But when you get saved, you're different. You have new desires; you have new want-tos in your

158

heart. You're different. How in the world can a person get run over by a MACK truck and not know it? How in the world can a person have something as glorious and wonderful as the great God of glory come into their heart and not know it and not be different? I hear some people who have the idea that they can walk down an aisle and have the preacher punch their ticket to heaven. Then they can walk out of church and live like the devil one day and go on to heaven the next. If you live like the devil, you're going to the devil.

A few years ago I was preaching a revival at Northview Baptist Church in Hillsboro, Ohio. On Monday night we had 3 people who were saved. There was a young lady about 20 years old and another woman about 40 years old. Then there was an older man who was 68 years old. He was the father of the 40-year-old lady who got saved. Understand what I mean by this: they were heathens. They had no church background whatsoever. They had been invited to the revival that night and God saved them. His name was Mr. Charlie. The next night we had 4 more people get saved. After the invitation was over, the pastor looked back and said, "Mr. Charlie, if you will, walk down here." I thought, that's one way to get another decision. He walked on down. The preacher said, "Folks, this is Mr. Charlie. Last night he got saved. God really saved him! This morning when I got to my office, Mr. Charlie was sitting on my doorstep. He said he needed to talk to me.

"He said, 'Pastor, last night, God truly saved me. But

there are some things that are true about my life that you don't know. Back in 1978, my wife and I got divorced, but I never moved out of the house. We just kept on living like we were still married. Last night after God saved me, I went home. I laid down in my bed and I knew things weren't right. I rolled and tumbled all night. I didn't want people to think I was a hypocrite. I want to come tonight and I want people to know God saved me, and I want to get things right.'"

There were 21 people saved during the revival that week and they all came back the next Sunday night to be baptized. Before they had the baptismal service, Mr. Charlie and his ex-wife came forward and the pastor married them. Then the pastor took them and baptized them! Folks, that's what happens when people really get saved! It's going to be revealed by their deeds, by their lives that they've been saved. Notice what these folks did in verse 19:

> *"Many of them also which used curious arts brought their books together, and burned them before all men: and they counted the price before them, and found it fifty thousand pieces of silver."*

When God saved them, they wanted to get anything and everything out of their lives that was wrong. They brought their books of curious arts, or books of black magic, or books of the occult. They piled them up and had a book burning service. Yes, sir, they wanted to burn everything out of their lives that would be wrong.

Let me quickly share with you a few things that you may need to let the Spirit of God burn out of your life.

- **Alcohol.** There are some of you who need to let God burn all beverage alcohol out of your life. I don't care if you've just been saved recently or for years. If you've got any beer in your refrigerator or any alcohol in your cabinets, you need to go home today and pour it down the toilet where it belongs. You don't need that ol' beer any longer. You don't need that ol' liquor any longer. You've got Jesus! Now don't be like the man who was at the church I used to pastor. His name was Larry. He was as green as a gourd. He'd been saved about 6 months. One Sunday I preached a message similar to this one— how if you got anything in your house that is wrong or would be a bad witness to you or your family, you need to get rid of it. On Wednesday night he came and knocked on my study door. I said, "Yes, Larry, come in." He said, "Preacher, you're going to be proud of me." I said, "Why's that, Larry?" He said, "You know you preached this last Sunday about whether we've got anything bad in our lives that would be a bad witness to our families. Well, I've been saved for about 6 months now. For about 6 months, I've had a can of beer in my refrigerator. I went home last Sunday and I got to thinking about it. When I saw that can of beer, I thought that's a bad witness to my children and I needed to get rid of it. So I just reached in, took it out, drank it and got rid of it!" I said, "Larry, that's not exactly the way you get rid of it." You're probably thinking, "Are you saying alcoholic beverages are bad?" That's exactly what I'm saying. I could give you Scripture after Scripture that speaks of the destruction and danger of alcoholic beverages.

- **Pornography.** Do you have some pornographic books in your home? If you do, you need to go home and have a book burning service. Or maybe you have some R-rated, X-rated videos. You need to go and, so to speak, have a book burning service. Some of you have HBO, Showtime, and Cinemax on your cable station. You need to make your way down to the cable station tomorrow and say, "I'm a Christian. I have no business having this in my home. I've asked God to forgive me and I want this removed before the sun goes down today." You'll never go on with God as long as you're feeding that trash into your mind.

- **All wrong music.** Some of you have secular rock music you need to get out of your life. Some of the young people are thinking, "I knew that ol' man wasn't going to be with it." I am prepared to show you why secular rock music is wrong. It's anti-God, anti-Christ, anti-authority, and anti-Bible. You'll never get on with God when you're feeding that trash into your mind. Let me tell you the reason a lot of folks don't get upset with their young kids listening to rock music: they can't understand the words. If you knew the words many of your children are listening to and putting into their minds, if you had ingrown toenails, they'd stand straight up. You say, "That's right, Preacher! Tell 'em about that rotten music!" Let me say something to you, Mommy and Daddy! If you've got any of that ol' dirty, filthy, country music, you're right there with the young people. Get it out of your life.

If you have anything in your life that keeps the name of Jesus from being magnified, you need to let the Holy Spirit burn it out of your life. Isn't amazing how we let so many things into our lives that keeps Jesus from being magnified? But let me tell you, when you turn your eyes on Jesus and look full in His wonderful face, the things of earth will grow strangely dim in the light of His glory and grace. When you get a clear vision of Jesus, you will say, "God, if there is anything wrong in my life, put Your finger on it. By Your grace, I'll get it out of my life. I want to be a holy man, a holy woman, a holy young person. I want to be a clean man, a clean woman, a clean young person. I want Jesus to be magnified." Do you want Jesus to be magnified through your life? Do you want to make much of the name of Jesus in your life? If you truly do, I believe God will show you exactly what has to take place in order for the name of the Lord Jesus to be magnified.

At the conclusion of every sermon I preached, I extended an invitation to the congregation to make a decision for Christ. I want to do the same with you now.

I want to ask you a very personal question: do you know that you know if you were to die right now you would be with God in heaven? Has there been a time and a place in your life where you have repented of your sin and trusted in Jesus Christ as your Savior and Lord? I am not asking you if you have been baptized. I am not asking if you have joined a church. But do you know that you have repented of your sin and trusted Christ as your Savior and Lord?

If you don't know that, you can pray this prayer. Make this your own personal prayer where you ask God to forgive you of your sin and trust Christ to save you.

"Dear God, I know You love me. I know Christ died on the cross for me. I know Christ came out of that grave and He is alive! But God, I have sinned against You. I am lost and I cannot save myself. God, I repent of my sin. Jesus, come into my heart and save my soul. Thank You, God, for saving me. I am going to live for You for the rest of my life. In Jesus' name I pray. Amen."

If you trusted Christ, I would love to hear from you so I can help you in your new life in Christ. You can contact me at:

Don Whitt

PO Box 12375

Jackson, TN 38308

Or email at: don@donwhitt.org

Welcome to the family of God!

ABOUT THE AUTHOR

D r. Don Whitt was born in Jefferson City, TN on July 27, 1950. He and his wife, Judy, have three sons and seven grandchildren. Judy lost her battle with cancer and complications in February 2015. Two of his sons serve as pastors: Brad in Augusta, GA, and Craig in Clinton, TN. His third, Paul, is a lawyer in Knoxville, TN.

Dr. Whitt received a Bachelor's of Arts degree from Carson-Newman College in Jefferson City, TN, a Masters of Divinity from Southwestern Baptist Theological Seminary in Fort Worth, TX and a Doctor of Ministry from Luther Rice Seminary in Lithonia, GA.

For over 30 years, Dr. Whitt has pastored churches ranging in size from 20 members to over 3,000 members. During that time, his messages have been broadcast throughout the southeastern United States. Dr. Whitt served as the State Evangelism Director for the state convention of Baptists in Ohio. He has preached over 1,000 local church revivals, several area wide crusades, state pastor's conferences, state evangelism conferences and college and seminary chapel services.

True to his Tennessee roots, Dr. Whitt is an avid quail hunter and has served as a professional hunting guide in some of the South's finest preserves.

Dr. Whitt has a heart for evangelism and the local church. God has particularly gifted him with the ability to call people to Christ and salvation.